Twenty Years Down the Mines

TWENTY YEARS
DOWN THE MINES

IAN TERRIS

STENLAKE PUBLISHING

This edition published in the United Kingdom, 2001,
by Stenlake Publishing, Ochiltree Sawmill, The Lade,
Ochiltree, Ayrshire, KA18 2NX
Telephone / Fax: 01290 423114
www.stenlake.co.uk

ISBN 1 84033 118 6

The cover photographs are reproduced courtesy of
Terry Harrison.

Printed in Great Britain by
Adlard Print & Reprographics Ltd,
Nottingham
www.adlardprint.com.

CONTENTS

ONE

CARDOWAN, 1952

My great-grandfather was a miner who worked in various parts of Fife and in 1859 my grandfather was born at Capledrae Colliery which was situated between Ballingry and Kinglassie. He married a Dunfermline lass and they set up home in Glasgow where he went to work as a metal planer at the locomotive works in Springburn. My father was a Corporation bus driver when he married my mother, who came from a district of Glasgow known as Gillshochill.

In 1937 I was born in Aitkenhead Road on the South Side of Glasgow, three storeys up in a tenement block overlooking Dixon's Blazes ironworks. When I was three years old my family flitted to Preston Street and I lived there until I was nineteen. I was educated at Calder Street Primary School and then at Queen's Park Secondary. I left with my leaving certificate when I was fifteen.

My interest in mining started at an exhibition in the Kelvin Hall. I can't remember the name of the exhibition but all kinds of industries took part and there was a mock pit on display. There was a corridor made to look like forests and as you walked along it, it showed how the forests died and then, over millions of years, turned to coal. I went down a lift made to look like a pit cage to a mock coal face with modern machinery. I can remember a machine that had moving arms at the front to load the coal on to a steel conveyor which emptied into a mine car.

When I was approaching fifteen I decided I wanted to be a mining engineer or mine manager so I wrote to the National Coal Board. I was interviewed by a gentleman called Mr Calder. He looked at the technical drawings I took with me and asked me what I wanted to do and how I thought I could achieve my goal. He explained what was involved in becoming a mine manager - it was not impossible but would require a lot of studies. Also, as well as working towards the qualifications, I would have to start work on the surface of a mine and work my way up the ladder. He then made me an offer to start on the tables at Cardowan Colliery, Stepps, as soon as I left school. That is where my story begins.

Having left secondary school on a Friday in April 1952, I found myself the following Monday morning standing at Killermont Street bus stance at six o'clock. I was waiting for the bus to take me to Cardowan Colliery and with me I carried an army kit bag containing my working clothes: bib and brace boiler suit, shirt, jacket, cap, socks and underwear. I also had with me a pair of shoes which my friend John Elliot, the street cobbler, had resoled with heavy tackets.

There were several men standing at the stance so I asked one of them which bus to take to Cardowan.

"Are you going to work there?" he asked me.

"Yes," I said, "I'm going to work at the tables."

A couple of them laughed, "Pity help you."

The bus came, a blue Alexander's double-decker whose destination board read 'Cardowan Colliery'. I boarded with a funny, excited feeling. The journey took us past Barlinnie prison, Hogganfield Loch, and along the main road past the Stepps stadium where they raced the trotting carts. We turned right off the main road towards Cardowan village and just before the village we turned left into the colliery. I got off the bus and walked through the big gates, looking around in total wonder. The pit offices were just inside the gates and opposite them was the pit canteen. One of the men asked me who I had to report to and when I told him, he showed me to the surface foreman's office.

The surface foreman was called John Clarke. Along with another wet-behind-the-ears school leaver, he took us into the pithead baths and showed us where to change into our working clothes. Then we reported back to his office and were taken to the time office to be issued with a round token called a check. A stern timekeeper gave instructions: "You collect this every morning before seven o'clock and return it here no earlier than 3.50 p.m. which is the official finishing time. You are responsible for this check - if you lose it you won't be paid."

Clarke then took us to the tables where stones were picked out of the coal before it was loaded into wagons. On the way we were able to have a look at the pit's yard. On the left was a large area called the woodyard, filled with wooden props, steel girders, pipes and other materials which some men were busy loading on to hutches for use underground. On the right of the yard was the lamp cabin where the miners got their lamps before going down the pit. I later found out there were two types of lamps: an electric one with a long cable and battery that you carried on your belt with the cap light fixed on to your helmet, and the flame safety lamp which was designed to give warning if gas was present underground. We also passed the engineering workshop and the blacksmith's shop where the miners' cutting tools were sharpened. Then we came to the pit-head, a steel structure with two large spoked wheels which towered high above.

It was a frosty spring morning. The sun was rising like an orange ball in the sky and its rays shone through the spinning wheels, creating a strange stroboscopic effect. The noise was tremendous. As the winding engine turned there was a chuffing noise like a train trying to gather speed and as the wheels turned faster, the noise grew louder. It was coming from the winding engines which were housed in a building opposite the pithead. Steel ropes came out of the winding engine house and, stretching over the winding wheels, were attached to the cages, one of which descended while the other ascended. The ropes were attached to the cages by a mechanism called the detaching hook which was designed to release the ropes from the cages in the event of the winder over-winding. A set of steel prongs would then automatically come out from the hook to prevent the cages from falling down the shaft.

The first shaft or pithead was called No.1 Shaft. This reached a depth of 1,800 feet and was the 'downcast' shaft, down which fresh air was drawn to ventilate the mine workings. I could see men and boys working together on the two levels of this pithead, pushing empty hutches into the cages and pulling the filled ones off. Cardowan had double-deck cages and the filled hutches ran down a gangway until they reached a creeper that took them to an area called the Hill. Thirty yards away stood No.2 Shaft which was 2,040 feet deep and was the 'up cast'. Its pithead was enclosed entirely within a concrete building and contained the large fans which drew the used air from the mine workings through the fan drift, allowing the fresh air to circulate.

Walking by the pitheads, I passed a steel stairway ascending to the Hill where the hutches of coal passed over the weighbridge. The weighbridge was necessary because the face workers (or strippers as they were called) were on tonnage payment. This meant that their section and hutch numbers had to be weighed and recorded so that they got paid appropriately. The hutches of coal then went onto the tumblers, a mechanical device that turned the hutches over to empty the coal out on to the tables below.

Passing under the Hill and the washer, where the dross and small coal was washed to get rid of any stones, I came to another stairway. I climbed up and walked along a steel gantry at the side of the wagons into a place that became fixed in my mind forever. It was a large windowless building, dark and dingy, and lit only by single bulb lamps hanging from a low roof. There was noise and dust everywhere. Boys of around my own age were bent double over clanking steel plate conveyors covered with coal. They were picking stones out of the coal and throwing them on to another conveyor belt that took them away to a hopper for the bing. In all there were three steel plate conveyors and one made of rubber. These were the screening or picking tables and were about thirty feet long and six feet wide. The boys also removed any stones that had coal attached to them (called 'parrot coal' in this pit) and these were broken up using a heavy hammer and sent to the washer to detach the coal.

At the top of each table there was a double steel shaker, a form of chute with holes in it to allow the dross and small coals to pass through on to the washer and above these were the tumblers on the Hill emptying the hutches of coal. The noise at the tables was tremendous and nobody could hear themselves think, let alone speak. But I was still excited - I was about to start my mining career.

Clarke handed us over to a rather fearsome looking man, the table gaffer, who had an old broken clay pipe, a 'jaw warmer', clamped in the side of his mouth. He spoke very gruffly and asked me for my can along with my tea and sugar container for the piece time brew-up. He then took me to one of the tables and handed me over to the man in charge there who set me to work alongside the other boys. There were three men at each table: one at the top at the shaker-end to operate the control levers to stop and start the table and two at the wagon-end to make sure no stones went into the wagons. We boys picked non-stop and the table gaffer had a habit of throwing a lump of coal at any of us who were not picking fast enough.

After about thirty minutes my hands were beginning to get numb from the ice-cold wind that came up from the wagon and my back was starting to ache with the constant bending. At ten o'clock everything stopped. It was piece time and I walked in line with the boys from my table up to the wagon-end. All our tea cans had been filled by the gaffer earlier and were now covered by a layer of black dust that had come off the coal dropping into the wagons from the tables above. We picked up our cans and then trooped into a brick hut. Once inside, the gaffer locked us in to "keep us out of mischief". Meanwhile, the men stayed in the main tables building where they were allowed to have their tea with the gaffer.

In the hut there was a roaring fire and some of the boys toasted their pieces using forks made out of belt wires. At quarter past ten the two Aberdeen express trains, *The Bon Accord* and *The Granite City*, passed by. One was going to Glasgow, the other to Aberdeen and these massive locomotives in the black and tan livery of the London, Midland & Scottish Railway were a sight to behold. Their passing meant that piece time was just about over. At twenty past ten the gaffer unlocked the door, hammering on it but not opening it. It was then back to picking stones again until two o'clock when everything stopped once more.

This stoppage was to wind the day shift miners up and let the back shift miners down. On this break we were allowed to go to the pit canteen which was beside the pithead baths. There I bought a third of a pint of milk and a Beatties snowball, which that day tasted better than any snowball I had ever had before. We then returned to the tables to pick stones until finishing time at ten to four when we went up to the check box to drop in our checks. After a hot shower in the baths and a change into clean clothes, I caught the bus and slept all through the journey before getting off to catch the tramcar to my street.

Next morning I awoke at quarter past five, aching all over with my hands covered in little cuts. On arriving at the pit baths I discovered that all my pit clothes, which I had left in the drying room as there were no lockers available, had been stolen. However, the bath attendant found me some old clothes and I went to the tables.

It was a cold morning and it wasn't long before my hands were frozen. The gaffer and the men were allowed to go up to the fire now and again for a heat, but not the boys. We had to ask permission to go to the toilet and frequently even this was refused. Once, one of the boys had an upset stomach and asked to go, but as usual the gaffer said no. The lad was leaning against the side of a table holding his stomach and when the gaffer threw a piece of coal at him, he had a rather unpleasant accident in his trousers.

It was like being in prison, and all for three pounds, two shillings and nine pence a week. One of the boys had the responsibility of filling the tea urn every morning and cleaning out the two eating places. He also had to kindle the fire in each place - at least there was no shortage of coal - and had to go to the manager's office to clean and polish his helmet, boots and gaiters when he came up from the pit. It was also said that he had to wash the manager's back. How true that was I don't know, but with that regime I wouldn't be at all surprised.

After a few weeks working at the tables, one day I was struck on the hand by a piece of coal. Looking up, I saw a boy pointing at me and then himself and clenching his fist.

"What does he want?" I asked the boy next to me.

"He wants to fight you," was the answer and when I asked why, I was told it was because I was different. "Do you know your nickname is 'Pardon'?" the boy said, "you never say 'whit?' or 'eh?' when you're asked a question."

"Okay," I called over to the boy wanting the fight, "when?"

"At the two o'clock break."

So, at two o'clock we went down past the wagons and up on to a lane that was outwith the pit boundary.

"Do you want a square go or all in?" my adversary asked me.

"Please yourself," I said.

"Right, we'll have a square go."

We squared up to each other and then all of a sudden he lowered his head and charged at me. He butted his head into my stomach but I got my arms around his waist, lifted him off his feet and threw him down the banking. "Watch your back Terris!" I heard and turning around I found the boy's mate charging down at me. Coming from the South Side, I used some rather dirty tactics and put him out of the fight. I jumped down to continue fighting the first boy and beat him with my fists, but then he kicked at me with his pit boots. I jumped back to avoid them and struck my head on a wagon's doors. Then the old wagon man appeared, charging at us with a brake stick and laying into us with it.

We were told to get back to the tables and as I was climbing up the stairs someone shouted, "Hey, Terris! Your heid's cut!" I ran my hand over the back of my head and I saw blood, *my blood*. The boy who I had been fighting was right behind me so I put my hands on the railings and jumping up, struck both my feet out behind me, hitting him squarely on the face and making a bit of a mess of it. The gaffer had a fit and sent us up to the surface foreman's office where we got a lecture about the dangers of fighting, especially in a pit. "It is a sacking offence," Mr Clarke said, "so shake hands and make friends or I'll sack the both of you." We shook hands and were pals from that day on.

After about six months of working in this hell hole, it was my turn to go and work on the Hill. What a difference I found in the attitude of the men who worked there - the gaffer even treated you like a human being! There were four work positions on the Hill. One was at the weighbridge, rubbing the numbers off the hutches; another was at the tumblers, on to which the hutches were guided so that the coal in them could be emptied onto the shakers; the third was also at the tumblers, removing the hutches from them and sending them down a gantry to return to the pithead; and the fourth place was at the redd tumbler ('redd' was any waste material extracted during mining operations). This was where I was sent and after spending six months at the tables, I was like a pit pony who had been released on to green pastures.

It was my job to get the redd hutches from the creeper (a slow moving endless chain with projecting bars to catch the axles of the hutches and haul them up from the pithead) and put them on to the redd tumbler. This emptied the contents of the hutches into a hopper which was used to fill the skips, which were themselves emptied on to the bing by means of their attachment to an aerial ropeway similar to a ski tow. I worked with Ronnie, the lad I had the fight with, and a man whose nickname was Smudger. Smudger spun many a yarn about his time in the army. He had no teeth but could bite and eat an apple quicker than the rest of us.

When we were not busy at the redd tumbler, we helped at the other positions. It was hard work - Cardowan was producing around 2,000 tons of coal a day so we were handling about 2,000 hutches. The workers on the Hill had their own hut to have their piece in and this had a pot-bellied stove in the middle of it. Just before piece time the boys feeding the tumblers would go and put the men's tin flasks of tea on the stove to heat, but they always had to remember to remove the stoppers from the flasks first. There was one grumpy man who was always getting at us, so one day we put his flask on the stove with the stopper still on, causing it to overheat and burst. Luckily there was nobody in the hut at the time, but we didn't half get a lecture from Frank the gaffer as well as getting our ears belted from the men.

Smudger was an excitable character and would rush to do whatever the gaffer said. At the redd tumbler we would put a wooden strap across the front of the hutches if we were going down into the hopper to clear any jammed stones. One day Ronnie and I saw that the hopper was jammed and putting the strap across the rails, we went in to clear it. Smudger was away having a fly smoke and didn't see us going in. Meanwhile, some hutches of redd were sent up from the pit and when the creeper started the hutches began to pile up. Frank shouted at Smudger to get the redd tumbler going so he removed the strap and started to empty the hutches. Ronnie and I heard the tumbler start up and it was lucky for us that there was also a chute down into the wagon in case the aerial ropeway broke down. We both slid down the chute into a wagon and climbed out.

After a short while Frank asked Smudger, "Where are Ian and Ronnie?"

"I don't know," replied Smudger, "I only took away the strap and started to empty the hutches."

"You took away the strap?" Frank asked.

"Yes," said Smudger.

Then the penny dropped. "You fool!" Frank shouted, "Ian and Ronnie are in the hopper." Everything was stopped and the men from the Hill all came climbing down into the hopper, looking for us and shouting our names. They even stopped the aerial ropeway and were frantically searching for us while we climbed back up the stair to the Hill.

Frank was standing at the tumbler, looking down. "What's wrong?" we asked him. Not looking at us, he replied "Ian and Ronnie are down there."

We asked again and this time he turned, "Ian and Ronnie are ... where the hell have you two been?"

"Down there," I said pointing down the hopper, "When the tumbler started up we slid down the chute into the wagon and have the cuts to prove it. Then we came up the stairs."

"Aye, but not before you had us searching for you." Frank said, belting us around the ears. "Thank God your all right. Now get back to work."

During my time as a young miner at Cardowan, I was allowed an allocation of two tons of coal a year. Half a ton at a time was dumped on the street outside my house and I had to carry it in buckets up a flight of stairs to put it in the coal bunker on the landing outside our door. The coal came from Garscube Colliery, the only mine left in Glasgow. It produced Cannel coal which was very easy to light and gave a great heat. This colliery was situated in Gillshochill where my mother came from and once, while visiting some relatives there, I decided to go and have a look at this mine with my younger brother, Gordon. It was a surface mine which was accessed by a tunnel rather than by a shaft and I was interested in seeing this. Nobody stopped us as we walked into the mine and we went down into the tunnel as far as we could. As there were no lights it was rather dark and Gordon was a wee bit scared. Later, we got a row from Mother because our shoes had got into a mess, but I was a young miner, enthusiastic about the job, and I wanted to see how other pits operated.

Two
Twechar, 1953

In January 1953 I was sent to Twechar to do my underground training. There were seven of us from Cardowan (although we were by no means 'magnificent') and we went by bus from Glasgow every morning, passing through Bishopbriggs and Kirkintilloch on the way. We also crossed the Forth and Clyde Canal by a bridge that was opened by hand to allow the boats to pass through.

The training pit was Gartshore No.10, although it was usually known as Twechar No.2 as it was the 'upcast' shaft for Twechar No.1 which was a coal producing pit. While we were there we did one day in the classroom and one day underground. On the first day we were rigged out in boiler suits, pit helmets and steel toe-capped boots, and given a talk by the manager who introduced us to our instructors and gave us a lecture about religion. There was to be no arguing or fighting about religion and no miscalling of anyone's beliefs. Anyone who was reported to him for doing this would be sent back to their own colliery and would not be trained for working underground, thereby making them liable for National Service. We all looked at him, a bit surprised. Although between us we numbered four Protestants and three Catholics, it had never occurred to us to argue about religion. We were Cardowan boys and that was that.

We were divided into two sections. My section was scheduled to go underground first and the next day we got our cap lamps from the lamp cabin and proceeded to the pithead. Arriving at Twechar's pithead was an experience exactly opposite to my arrival at Cardowan. This was the upcast for Twechar No.1, but all I could see was a small set of winding wheels above a wooden platform. Running through holes in this platform were the ropes attached to the cages. Even the winding engine house was small and the boiler house was a one-man affair. The boiler stoker doubled as the banksman, whose job it was to load and unload the cage either with men or hutches.

When the cage arrived we clambered into it with some apprehension as none of us had been underground before. The cage was smaller than the ones at Cardowan and only six boys could get in along with an instructor who had to bend down to enter it. The banksman closed the cage gates and signalled to the winding engine operator who then lowered us down the shaft. The cage descended slowly and just below the surface it stopped right opposite the fan drift. The damp mine air was rushing into the fan and we got soaked - now we knew why the instructors all wore oilskin jackets. This was our introduction to Twechar, the instructor informed us. Then suddenly the cage dropped like a stone, hurtling downwards, and all we could see was the lights from our cap lamps shining on the sides of the shaft as we sped below.

A few moments later we arrived at the pit bottom. On leaving the cage with knees shaking, I was surprised to see how brightly lit the pit bottom was. It was even whitewashed to make it brighter. We were taken into an underground 'howf' (or office) and here were allocated our various tasks. All the Cardowan boys were put together to learn how to use 'lashing chains', a six foot chain with a hook at one end and a large link at the other, for attaching groups of hutches on to the haulage system. This was a steel rope system that moved continuously while the coal face loaders were in full production and we had to learn how to attach these chains to the moving steel rope. The method was to attach the large link to the drawbar of the hutch and then place the hook at the other end of the chain over the moving steel rope. Turning the hook and chain around the rope for three or four turns, the chain would then tighten around the rope and, linked together like this, they would pull a group of hutches off towards the coal loading point which could be a mile or more away.

We were also instructed in the use of haulage clips such as the Smallman, Bulldog and Hambone, which in some circumstances were used instead of the lashing chains, and were also taken to a non-productive coal face for an insight into the type of work done by a faceman. This face was only two feet, six inches high.

Previous trainees had, over a period of time, dug away the soft section at the foot of the seam and the instructors had stacked this coal at the ends of the face, which were known as gate ends. We were given the pleasant task of taking empty hutches into the gates, loading them with this coal by hand, and then pushing the full ones out to the haulage rope and bringing in the empties. We were split into two squads. The other group were boys from the Kilsyth area and, inevitably, there was a bit of rivalry between us. Each squad got up to a few tricks to hinder the other - we stole a set of their rails and hid them, and they retaliated by derailing our hutches out at the haulage.

Eventually we got twelve hutches out to the haulage system where they were drawn away towards Twechar No.1 to be sent to the surface. We thought that the haulage took the hutches all the way, but we were in for a surprise as we had to go and push them through a length of tunnel for several hundred yards and then through ventilation doors and down an incline to No.1 pit bottom. Here we had a slight mishap as the hutches ran away from us and collided with some stationary ones waiting at the pit bottom. Several of the hutches were derailed and we were made to lift them back on to the rails and clean up the spillage by hand. The pit bottomer was not a happy man and we were not, as he called us, his favourite "blankity-blank trainees".

At the Twechar training pit we were taught many aspects of working underground, including rope splicing (joining steel ropes together) and turning hutches on steel plates which acted as a turntable. When a cage landed in the pit bottom, the pit bottomer loaded the bottom deck first with a full hutch and in the process knocked the empty hutch off on to steel plates. A lad would turn the hutches around on these swivelling plates and then couple them on to the rope haulage which would take them out to the face loader. This operation would be repeated for the top deck of the cage and so on for the rest of the shift. Such a system was useful in pits like Twechar where there was a lack of space and no room for rails for the hutches.

In the classroom we were taught mining theory along with mathematics and science. We were also taught first aid and received a certificate for this. Physical training was given by an ex-army instructor who really put us through our paces. In the school we were assessed for further education and I passed to attend day release classes after completion of my training. During our sixteen weeks at Twechar we also had to work every second Saturday at Cardowan, either at the pithead or on the Hill depending on where extra hands were needed.

We had many escapades during our time at Twechar. To get to the training pit you had to cross a bridge over the Forth and Clyde Canal which had a hand operated opening centre section which allowed the boats to sail between the Forth and Clyde rivers. Everyday we went to the canteen at Twechar No.1. This was five hundred yards along the main road to Kilsyth and there was always a race to get there between those who were underground and those from the classroom. One day we were in the classroom and got a head start on the lads from underground. Crossing over the bridge, someone suggested we raise it to slow the others down. So we raised the bridge and went off to eat, but we forgot that the only hand-operated cranking wheel to lower the bridge was on the canteen side and the other lads had to wait until a motorist stopped and lowered the bridge for them to get across. There was a bit of a scrap when they finally caught up with us.

Another day we were underground and when we came to the surface for our piece time we noticed a repair barge tied up at the bank of the canal. The workers had gone off for lunch and we decided that it would be a nice change to sail to the canteen instead of walking. Clambering aboard we cast off and away we went like Vikings, only we were wearing mining helmets instead of horned ones. Suddenly the wind blew one lad's helmet off into the water and he made a grab for it, stepping out over the edge of the barge. Luckily for him we had a big lad with us who caught him by the scruff of his boiler suit or he would have joined his helmet at the bottom of the canal. This got us a rather long lecture from the fireman, both on losing the helmet and for taking the workmen's barge away.

In the tunnel leading to No.1 pit bottom where the rake of hutches had run away from us, we were to install a rope haulage system. Along the side of this tunnel, and running along its whole length, a two feet high wall had been built about three feet out from the side to carry water from the mine workings to the pump house where it was pumped to the surface. We were there with an instructor and he was splicing the steel rope. (This involved joining, or butting, the two ends of the rope together by removing the hemp rope core and using metal rods called spoons to splice the strands in where the core had been removed.) After butting the two ends together, the instructor started splicing and we held the single strands of the rope apart to accommodate the intertwining of the rope. The instructor told one of the lads to move over to his right. He did this but the instructor kept telling him to go further yet until a noise made us look over at him. There he was, standing up to his waist in the freezing cold water. We thought the instructor was going to have a fit and you can imagine the ribbing we gave him.

Another time we were whitewashing the walls and roof of the pit bottom area and we decided to have a small battle using our brushes to throw the paint at each other. This was fun for a while but then we decided to liven things up a bit and catch one of the lads with the remains of the paint bucket. We hid behind the steel plates covering a haulage return wheel in the middle of the tunnel and as soon as we heard the lad coming we let him have it with the bucket. But instead of the lad, we had covered the fireman from head to foot. We were in deep trouble, but were given a choice: either report to the manager or take the fireman's punishment. We opted for the latter so after piece time we returned underground and were taken to an old section of the mine that had a two foot high coal face and a sump full of evil-smelling water. At the side of this sump there was a handpump, like the type you use on a small boat to pump out the bilge, and our punishment was to pump this water out as they were going to use this face as a training face for No.1 pit. For the next few underground days, we were taken there first thing in the morning and spent the whole shift there, stopping only for lunch, and then back again. I discovered muscles on my body that I didn't know existed.

On the non-productive coal face we were taught how to put up wooden pit props using a hammer called a hawk (a pick-headed hammer also used to dig out coal), and how to remove pit props from the waste after the coal has been dug out, using a steel chain and a ratchet type of apparatus called a sylvester that was anchored to the coal face. This was used so that miners did not have to go into an unsafe place to remove props or girders. We were also shown how to build wooden pillar supports, which stood from the floor to the roof and contained a steel release mechanism to make them easier to dismantle before moving to a new position on the face. Four feet or more was dug off a coal face every shift, so face conveyors had to be moved and gate ends had to be brushed (to remove part of the roof in order to heighten the tunnel), so pillar supports were constantly moved.

Another task was to get the training face for Twechar No.1 ready and we even installed a coal-cutting machine. It was during this installation that our instructor told us a strange tale. A friend of his was a fireman in the Gartcosh pits which were known as Gracehill Nos.9 and 10, and 3 and 11. Two were still in production and two were out of use, although there were still links between them which were to be used as escape routes should anything happen. At week-ends this fireman had to go through these workings and come up one of the non-productive pits and when he was leaving he would contact the engine room to let them know that he was on his way through so that a cage would be ready for him. One day the winding engine man was duly phoned by the fireman and a cage was sent down to get him. Then the cage bells rang and rang before abruptly falling silent. The winding engine man very slowly raised the cage to the surface and found the fireman lying unconscious on its floor. He was carried into the winding house and when he came round he told how he was walking along the abandoned haulage road when a strange feeling came over him and he felt the hairs on his neck start to rise. A strange glow seemed to approach him and within it he could see a woman with a basket strapped on her back and around her head. In her arms she carried a small boy whose lit-tle body was broken and bloody as if he had been crushed. Tears ran down the woman's face. The fireman stood transfixed as she walked past him and disappeared into the side of the roadway. Absolutely terrified, he ran to the cage and once inside it he just pulled and pulled on the bell before he passed out.

One of my enduring memories of Twechar was of the pump house at No.1, spotlessly clean with whitewashed walls. On these walls hung pencilled and coloured drawings of miners digging coal and pushing hutches and of pit ponies both underground and in green fields above. They were all works of art, drawn by the pumper who had no tuition in drawing and was a natural artist.

When we went to the canteen we used to see a lad walking about with a wooden strap balanced on his head. We asked the canteen lady who he was and she said he was a local lad who was mentally retarded and walked about like that all day. She told us that the miners got their pay in a bowl and after checking it, they were supplied with an envelope to put it in. At the side of the pay window sat an empty envelope and the miners would drop into it the odd penny or threepenny piece. After all the miners were paid, the wages clerk would take in the envelope and the lad would then come up to the window. From this envelope he would get his pay counted out into a bowl and get his own envelope to take it home in. That's what I call really taking care of your own.

THREE

CARDOWAN, 1953 - 1954

After my stint at Twechar I returned full-time to Cardowan and was sent to work at No.2 pithead, removing the hutches from the top deck. Cardowan's cages had two decks and each one held two one ton hutches. When the cage landed the banksman would push two empty hutches on to the cage. My job at the back of the cage was to raise an iron bar at the side of the cage (this bar prevented movement of the hutches during the ascent and descent of the cages) and stand on a pedal on the floor to release another safety device. Then, pulling the two full hutches off the cage, I pushed the hutches through two sets of ventilation doors as No.2 was the upcast shaft. Remembering to close the doors behind me, I would push the hutches out to the foot of the creeper that would take them to the Hill. If I forgot to close a set of doors the others would open with the weight of the hutches then slam shut due to the force of the air trying to get into the fan and crush my legs and ankles. This only happened once or twice and I didn't forget again - it was rather a painful lesson to learn.

No.2 pit stopped winding coal at two o'clock everyday and we were then sent to help wherever we were needed. I was sent out to the empty wagon sidings, assisting the pug driver and his shunter to set the empty wagons into the four lanes of the tables for filling. Then we would take the full wagon to the main sidings where they were organised into trains for the larger main line locomotives to haul away to steelworks or cokeworks where the gas was extracted from the coal. (Cardowan's coal was coking coal and it was a very gassy pit to work in. It was nicknamed 'the Gasometer'.) During this operation with the pug, the driver would let me drive up and down to the sidings and this same pug was later donated by the NCB to a children's play area in Dunfermline Glen, Fife.

On the pithead I worked with three other lads, one of whom,

Charlie, who worked the bottom deck, was a great Nat King Cole fan and sang his songs all day long. His favourite was 'I will never change, I'll always love you'. Two men supervised us: one on the top deck and on the bottom deck, the main banksman, Mr Barclay, who was in charge of the signal bells for sending the cages away. We boys took turns to go to the blacksmith's shop to brew up the tea cans on the fire for piece time. The six cans were boiled over the fire but Mr Barclay's had to be boiled a couple of times until it looked and tasted like tar. If you got it wrong he sent you back to get it right.

While I was working on the pithead the surface foreman, still Mr Clarke, sent for me. He had a special job for me to do. I was to go around the pithead railway sidings and take the numbers of all the internal wagons. They all carried the name of the private company who used to own the pit before nationalisation - Dunlop - and beside this they had their individual number stencilled on the side. He wanted to record the number of wagons that were still serviceable and I spent a few happy weeks on and off the pug and in and out of parts of the pit that previously I hadn't known existed.

After this I was put into the stores as an assistant and as I had been taught at school how to use a nib and ink for writing, I was given the task of writing up a new stores register as well as issuing store items to the miners. Part of my stores job was to fill tin boxes with explosives and to prepare the shotfirers' detonator bags. There was no true record kept of what went where and over a period of days I smuggled home three detonators and a couple of cartridges of explosives. There was a place nearby called the Mall's Mire, a large area of land that was mainly boggy, and the slag from Dixon's Blazes blast furnaces was taken there in large steel side-tipping railway wagons. Sometimes the slag would spill out of the wagons like molten lava while other times it would come out in one large, dome-shaped lump.

Early one evening my pal and I, armed with the flex of an old electric lamp and a double battery from the front light of my bike, went there to have some fun with my plunder. Placing a small piece of explosive and a detonator under one of the domes, we hid behind the one next to it and set off the explosive. There was a loud crack and the dome split in two. We thought this was great and set off to the Queen's Park recreation ground. Beside the pavilion we dug in and buried three ounces of explosives with a detonator. We then hid round the side of the pavilion and set it off, sending clods of grass and earth flying in all directions. We emerged from our hiding place covered in earth and muck to find we had made a very large hole in the ground, so we ran off for dear life.

For a few days we laid low, hiding the remainder of the explosive and the detonator in an air raid shelter. Then I decided to get rid of them and took them down to the back court of the tenement where I lived. I dug a hole by the side of one of the brick-built middens and set up the charge. Setting it off, I scurried back inside the tenement and I was in the house before the noise had stopped, looking out the window with everyone else. I then went out to empty my mum's rubbish and all the people were out looking around the foot of the tenement, talking about the debris hitting their windows and trying to find out where it had come from. By this time it was dark and I went to the spot where I had set off the explosive to find a large hole in the ground. Panicking, I quickly pushed muck back into the hole while trying to keep people from seeing me as I levelled it off. I was very lucky not to get caught. If I had, my mining career would have been finished before it even got started. I might also have landed in 'Bar L' for a spell.

During my time in the stores I explored a lot more of the surface of Cardowan. One of the places I got to was the winding engine house of No.2 shaft. It was something to see - the floor was spotless and all the brass work around the various working parts of the engine was shining bright. The large steam engine operated pistons on either side and they moved on a shaft turning the huge drum that held the steel winding ropes. When these pistons moved in and out, the shaft started to rotate the drum, making the cages ascend and descend (as one cage descended within the pit shaft the other one ascended). As the drum rotated faster and faster a circular indicator marked in fathoms showed where the cages were in the shaft. When the cages reached the surface mark on the indicator, the winding engine man stopped the engine to allow the cages to be unloaded.

The operation of this large steam engine was very impressive. The winding engine man sat on a chair at the three control levers, the brake, the throttle and the direction lever. He sat with his feet on a bar and pulled the brake off and held it in the crook of his arm (should he have for any reason let go of this lever it sprung back to the 'brake on' - or 'dead man' - position). Once he had the brake in his arm, he set the control lever over and then pulled the throttle slowly towards himself to increase the speed. He pulled on the throttle more and more until the engine was at full speed and the indictor was moving round. When the indicator showed mid-shaft he eased off the throttle until the two cages passed so as to avoid any collision between them at high speeds. He then increased speed once more until they reached the surface. I visited the engine house quite a lot and was allowed to operate the engine once or twice to bring up hutches. There were two speeds on the engine - one for men and a faster one for materials.

Next to the winding engine houses was the boiler house, a large brick building containing twelve or more Lancashire boilers along one side with dross hoppers standing opposite them. Here the stokers shovelled the dross from the hoppers into the fire boxes of the boilers to produce the steam that powered the two winding engines. The boilers were worked twenty-four hours a day, every day of the year, as even on the days when the pits were not producing coal the firemen still had to go down and inspect them to check for gas. The boiler house made me think of Dante's Inferno. It was so hot and dirty it was known as the 'firehole' and the stokers didn't get much respite during their shift with the pit winding hell for leather.

During this time I also got friendly with one of the blacksmiths who was deaf and dumb. He was from Glasgow like myself and we used to talk using signs and chalk on the floor. He was great at his work and when I became a face worker later on I always went to him to get my tools sharpened. He would put the tool in the fire and watch the steel turning different shades according to its temperature. This would guide him on when to remove the tool from the fire and hammer it on the anvil, and he would move it back and forth between fire and anvil, hammering away until he was satisfied the tool was ready. Then he would submerge it in oil to harden it.

I had spent a good part of my time in the stores, writing up the new stores ledger, when one day the training officer came to see me. He wanted me to stay put until I was eighteen before sending me underground, but I told him I wanted to go down when it was my turn. So, two days later I was sent out to work at the pithead once more and a few weeks after that I went underground to work for the first time, a boy of sixteen.

Four

Cardowan, 1954 - 1956

I was fortunate to be sent down No.2 pit, the better pit of the two which, although gassier, was warmer. No.1 was the downcast shaft. In winter ice would form on the sides of the shaft and would crash down on top of the cages so large fires were lit at the pithead to heat the air going down the shaft. The boys who worked the pit bottom in this shaft were not supplied with warm clothing and had to buy their own. A pair of moleskin trousers cost you two pounds and four shillings and as they got little more than that for wages, they went on strike. The manager then consented to give them some protective clothing and supplied them with balaclavas. Big deal. Some years later they got duffel coats. It was so cold that some of the strippers even wore cut-down army greatcoats. Every Spring the two cages had to be replaced because they were all bent and buckled by the ice.

I started in the pit bottom area at the top of the empty creeper. My first job was to couple the hutches together using coupling chains. I had to be quite nippy as the creeper was bringing hutches up all the time and as they pushed into each other I had to watch that I didn't get my head caught between them. After coupling them into rakes or groups of twelve I pushed them into a tunnel. I did this for a week and then was sent to push them through two sets of steel ventilation doors (No.2 was the upcast shaft and had ventilation doors around the pit bottom to allow the fans to draw the used air up the shaft). I pushed the rake of hutches down the tunnel for a distance of about five hundred yards to the main haulage and they were then taken by overhead rope haulage to the faces which were about two miles away.

This was very hard and strenuous work. There were two of us and the tunnel rose upwards about a hundred yards from the end. When the loader was in full production and the hutches were disappearing away on the haulage rope it took us all our time to keep up with the rakes required. Sometimes the hutch wheels were stiff and needed to be oiled. Sometimes we were actually pushing on the bumpers, bent double with our feet hard on the rail sleepers to keep the momentum up. I soon developed healthy leg muscles.

After four weeks of this I was put on the backshift (2 p.m. - 10 p.m.) to allow a lad on this shift to move to dayshift. I was sent into a section called the Main East which was the main section with other sections being worked off from it. Cardowan's method of mining coal was known as the 'long wall' method, a system of mining involving complete excavation at one working. I was put at the junction between 2 East and the Main East where the belts joined and my job was to work the engine for the conveyor belt which fed on to the main trunk belt. This belt went out to the loader to fill the hutches.

The backshift was the preparatory shift, beginning after all the coal had been stripped for the day, and the first task was to move the conveyors to the face. The tail gates and the main gate brushing was carried out after these operations so the surplus redd was shovelled on to the belt and sent to the loader to be transported out to the pit bottom and sent to the surface. I then had to take pit props and girders into the face to the face workers (who were known as brushers). Often the fireman, Jock, would slip a few extra payments on to the time book if I took in some heavy girders to the face. Sometimes I would accompany him up the face with some props for the brushers that brushed the small roads in the face. These were called dummy roads because they never went anywhere and were allowed to cave in behind the face. The debris from this brushing was used for packs in the middle of the face to help support it.

This face was only eighteen inches high and was supported by wooden props which creaked and groaned as the weight of the roof began to press down on them. Sometimes they actually split and had to be replaced. My method was to throw about two dozen props in front of me, crawl up to them on my belly and throw them forward once more, and so on until I reached the brushers. One day as I was doing this I was chewing gum and cracking it between my teeth. Jock told me to stop doing this as the roof was making crack-ing noises and some of the props were splitting. He needed to listen carefully to make sure everything was all right. A little way up the face I forgot and did it again. Again he told me to stop. Then I for-got and did it once more, so he gave me a skelp across the ear. I swallowed the gum at once because I didn't fancy another one.

One time when I was at my belt engine, I could smell burning coming from the loader so I told Jock and we went to investigate. When we reached the loader all we could see was pieces of redd all over the place and no sign of the lad who was supposed to be work-ing the loader. We looked around and found him fast asleep on a platform that had been built into an old tunnel. The loader lads usually had their piece in there to keep out of the draughty air com-ing past. Jock grabbed the lad and shook him like a rag doll. Then he gave him a row, telling him to clear up the mess and daring any-one else to help him. By that time more of the lads had come out to see what was wrong with the belts. The lad was lucky because not only was sleeping down the pit a sacking offence, he could also have been prosecuted for it.

One day another fireman called John Lowden came to see me at my belt engine. He wanted to know where I went to do the toilet during my shift. There were no toilets underground in those days and I was a little embarrassed by the question so said I usually went when I was on the surface. "Everybody goes when they're underground at sometime or other," he said, "Anyway, I'll show you where you must never go."

We went into the main return airway and walked to another junc-tion in the tunnels (or 'roads' as they were called) where an old tun-nel joined the return. This tunnel had a wire mesh across the entrance and a 'No Entry' notice attached to it. The fireman took his flame safety lamp and, turning it down to a very low flame, put it against the mesh and put his cap lamp off, telling me to do like-wise. I noticed a long blue cone shape rising above the testing flame. This, he told me, was firedamp gas burning inside his lamp. There was about five percent in the air, a dangerous amount which could explode in the tunnel and ignite any coal dust that was there, causing an even bigger explosion. Years ago this had happened in

Cardowan in a section known as the Dooks. Several men had lost their lives and the entrance to the section was bricked-up. He told me that I was never to go into this old road - there was no oxygen in there and after only a few steps I would collapse and die.

While I was at this section I was treated like a son by some of the men and they used to keep a part of their piece for me as I was always hungry. Jock was also good to me. One day when I was cleaning out the bottom of the belt, a large piece of redd broke in my hand and crushed my pinky, ripping off the nail. I ran into the face about three hundred yards away holding my hand, blood seeping through my fingers. When I reached the face, Jock was there and he told me to sit down and got one of the brushers to give me a drink of water. There were no taps or drinking water down a coal mine and you had to carry your own in a tin flask or a glass lemon-ade bottle. The brusher gave me a drink out of his flask while Jock bandaged my finger. Then he sent me up to the medical room at the pithead baths. The next day I had to go to the hospital where they cut off what remained of the nail and signed me off work for a few weeks.

During these weeks I still went to the pit to get my wages and my brother Gordon always came with me. One time I took him along to the No.1 pithead just as the dayshift miners were coming up. We were standing at the shaft gates on the bottom level where it was quite dark by the time the cage arrived. Suddenly there was the crashing of the chains lifting the shaft gates and the miners threw open the internal gate, shouting at one another as they emerged from the cage. Their lamps shone from their helmets and the whites of their eyes glowed from faces as black as the Earl of Hell's waistcoat. They scared the living daylights out of my brother and I don't think he ever forgave me.

It was during my spell on the backshift that I saw how men's reactions differed during alarming situations. There was one brusher who was built like a mountain and was as hard as nails, or so we all thought. One Sunday we were going underground and the guide ropes on the cages had just been changed. As we started to descend the new ropes gave a high-pitched scream which was a bit frightening. This brusher, alarmed at the racket, was convinced that the cages were running out of control and he tried to open the cage gates to jump out. The rest of the brushers had to hold him back and by the time we got to the bottom he was so frightened he was shaking like a leaf.

After a spell at the face loaders, I went to work at the pit bottom for a short time before moving to the dayshift nine months later. At the pit bottom I uncoupled the full hutches and fed them into the lanes for entry on to the cages. As they came out from both the east side and the west side, I had to watch that they did not collide and controlled them by using snibbles, an iron bar which was used as a brake by inserting it into the spokes of the hutch wheels. The rakes of hutches coming from the east were made up of five hutches while the rakes coming from the west were made up of twelve hutches, so our work was cut out for us keeping everything running smoothly.

After a short period spent uncoupling hutches in the pit bottom, I was sent into the west side where I took rakes of twelve full hutches off the rope haulage and, again using snibbles, I sent them through the ventilation doors to the pit bottom. The hutches were released from the haulage and after slowing them down with the snibbles, I would knock on the blast pipe to let the lad at the pit bottom know that a rake was on its way through. If the pit bottom was full he would ring once on a bell and I would stop the rake and others coming off the haulage. Then, when the pit bottom was ready to take my rakes, he would ring twice on the bell and I would start to send them through.

I had a pal called Lachie who worked in No.1 doing the same task. As mentioned before, this was a very cold pit and he told me that he was fed up with the conditions and wanted to leave the job. I told him if he left he would get called up for National Service, but he said he had a plan to avoid this. He had a plan all right, the idiot, and it involved letting a full hutch run over the index finger of his right hand. Anyway, he went to hospital and although his finger healed all right, it was permanently bent and he couldn't straighten it. He left the pit shortly afterwards and was duly called up for an army medical which he passed 'A1'. In desperation, Lachie showed the medical officer his bent finger. The officer was very sympathetic and gave him a pen to sign his name. Lachie took the pen in his bent finger and signed his name. The officer said, "Well done lad, you can write okay. I'll put you in the Pay Corp." Poor Lachie. As far as I heard he actually had a good time in the army and he came to see us once at the pit gates, dressed in his uniform.

After a spell of this 'tunnel running' as it was called, I was sent to a new section that was being developed to produce a high grade of coking coal. It was called Five West and the face was eighteen inches high. I was there to work the loader, sending the hutches of coal down a steep incline of one in five to be transferred on to the main haulage at No.2 West. This haulage at No.2 West was known as a cuddie brae. The weight of the full hutches going down pulled the empty ones up and the system was controlled by a man operating a brake on the wheel that the rope went around. There were about two hundred full hutches on this system, arranged into rakes of four.

There were five of us to work this loader. The haulage man was nicknamed Chappie as he always called everybody he talked to 'Chappie'. He was a character - one day he turned up for work in a set of tails that someone had given him. My immediate workmate was called Joe and he was a great dog-racing man who ran his own dog - I even won a few bob on it. Along with us there were two other lads, John and Willie, both from the Hamilton area.

We had a large haulage engine positioned above our loader and this was going to replace the cuddie brae when this section went into full production. The steel rope on this engine had a habit of twisting in on itself and you had to watch you didn't catch any loose clothing on it when a bulldog clip carrying a rake of empty hutches was released on arrival at the loader level. As we were only a developing section, we did not have sufficient bulldog clips to take the rakes right up to the back of the loader to be placed behind the hopper to get filled. We therefore had to use a smallman clip to push them up. This clip was placed behind the group of twelve hutches and was able to push all twelve up to a set of spring points, getting four over the points and down to the loader at a time. The remaining eight ran back down and the clip had to push them up again until another four went over, and so on until all twelve hutches

were at the loader. One day as Joe was pushing the hutches up in
this manner the rope twisted and caught his jersey, pulling him
over five hutches before the jersey gave way and he dropped into
one. He was a bit scraped but otherwise all right. We kept getting
on to the overman about this but all he would say was that the
bulldog clips were on order.

The face continued to be developed, additional strippers were
employed on it, and the amount of hutches being filled increased.
One Saturday Joe wasn't at work and an older man, from another
loader, was sent to take his place. He saw the way we were taking
up the empties four at a time and decided to revert back to the old
system of taking twelve together. We tried to tell him that the clip
wouldn't hold them but he was adamant so we left him to get on
with it. On his third attempt to get his first twelve hutches up, the
rope twisted and caught his shirt, dragging him over the whole
twelve hutches before the haulage managed to stop. His arm was
only inches away from the pulley wheel at the entrance to the
haulage house and when we got to him we had to cut his shirt away
to release him. The side of him that had been dragged over the
hutches looked as if someone had taken a giant cheese grater up
and down it. The fireman came out and gave him first aid and, as
we put him on the stretcher, he kept saying, "I'll be all right to work
on Sunday as usual." We finally got the new clips a couple of days
later.

A few weeks later the face went into full production and my job
was to write on the hutch the section name - '5W' - and the hutch
number so that the weigh man could record the tonnage for the
strippers. They were paid thirty-four shillings and eleven pence a
shift, plus five shillings and three pence for every ton that they dug.
There were seventeen strippers on each side of the coal face and all
their coal came out to the loader on a main trunk belt. We filled
about five hundred hutches per shift and we also had to take hutches of props and girders off the main haulage and push them into the
main gate for the supply laddies to take into the face. One day, as
the loader was working at top speed and we were struggling to keep
it supplied with empties, I was down below the main gate writing
the numbers on the side as they came along the straight. Someone

had left the switches open and suddenly, when I wasn't expecting them, the hutches turned into the main gate and crushed me against the side of the tunnel. I could feel the breath being squeezed out of me and I shouted at Joe to stop the haulage. I felt my hips being crushed and thought I'd had it when suddenly I found myself standing on the opposite side of the main gate and about twenty feet away from the rake of hutches which had just been crushing me. Joe came running down as I was inspecting my bruised hips.

"See you, you bastard!" he cried, "You've got a guardian angel!"

I asked what he meant and he said, "When you shouted on me I looked down and saw two figures at the tunnel side being crushed by the hutches. But when I belled off the haulage there was nobody in there and you were standing where you are now." Neither of us could explain it and I never could work out how I managed to escape from the situation. Maybe I really did have a guardian angel.

While I worked at this loader, I used to sit in a manhole (a refuge at the side of a tunnel which miners can occupy while hutches pass by) to have my piece at ten o'clock. One day a little mouse appeared and sat looking at me. I threw him a bit of bread and just like a squirrel he picked it up between his paws and ate it. I called him Hector and every day, regular as clockwork, he appeared for his tit-bit and went off again before the loader restarted at twenty past. He kept me company for a while and then one day he didn't appear. I missed him a lot. Miners like mice because, like the canaries, their breathing rate is about four times as fast as humans. If there was any gas about such as whitedamp (the mining term for carbon monoxide) they would keel over, giving you the warning to get out. Also, if you saw a mouse trying to climb up props or try to reach high ground, then there was water about and you were extra careful in case of an inrush. Two miners had been killed when this had happened a number of years before.

Our overman was a character. His greatest possession was a pocket watch that he kept in a round tin. "See this watch," he would tell anyone who was around, "it was the only thing still going when my father fell down Auchengeich shaft." Apparently his father had been a shanker (a man in charge of the upkeep of the shaft) and had fallen to his death. His watch was found still working and had been given to his son.

A short time before the loader came into full production, I was sitting along with Jack the roadsman at the top of the incline when I heard a faint shout for help. Jack thought it was just the water in the compressed air pipes, but I was sure it was somebody shouting. We went down the incline to investigate and saw a lamp shining under a rake of hutches. We ran on and came upon a lad whose arm was caught between the rope and the chain of the bulldog clip. The lad had been fixing the rope on top of the hutches when it twisted, trapping his arm. He was convinced his arm was off because he couldn't see it or feel it as the circulation had been cut off. We released the chain and he fell down holding his arm. Then the pins and needles started with a vengeance as the circulation returned. I discovered it was my mate Ronnie from the redd tumbler. He had come down the pit a little while after me and he was lucky I had heard his shout or he might have lost his arm. What a way to meet up again!

Five

Cardowan, 1956 - 1957

I worked at the loader until September 1956 and was then sent to the training face to learn how to dig coal and become a stripper. The training lasted for eighty days and was based at the training face opposite No.2 West section. Here young miners were taught the duties of the faceman, a job title that could incorporate the tasks of stripper, brusher and belt shifter. My supervisor was a man named Hugh who had been a POW during the Second World War. He had been sent to work in salt mines which apparently had been a horrendous experience. He was a great supervisor and we got on well.

The training seam was eighteen inches high and was supported by wooden props. The coal was dug out using compressed air picks known as puggers. We were supposed to start stripping a 'man's stint' of twenty feet and progress up to thirty feet, but I just started at thirty feet and that was that. To dig out the coal I had to lie on my side on top of my shovel and dig away with the pugger to loosen it off and then lie on a pit prop to shovel it on to a bottom-load belt which ran the length of the face, taking the coal to the main gate trunk belt which in turn took it out to the loader. My knuckles and shoulders were soon skint due to striking them off the low roof. I learned to wear gloves to save my hands, but there was nothing I could do about my shoulders as all we wore were peewits, singlets usually made of blue/grey flannel, the colour of a lapwing's wings.

At the start of a shift it took us around thirty minutes to walk from the pit bottom to the main gate of the training face where we waited for the fireman to give us our tasks. These consisted of face stripping, tail gate and main gate brushing, conveyor shifting or supplying the face with props and girders. We all had to take our turn at the latter. Our place on the face was at the top end near the tail gate. Hugh and I stripped our thirty feet and set wooden props four feet apart and no more than three feet from the face. This was in compliance with the Coal Mines and Quarries Act which we were governed by. The tail gate required a different type of brushing from the main gate, known as pavement brushing (i.e. enlarging a roadway by taking away from the floor). We had to bore four holes in the pavement using a compressed air percussion borer. This was done without a water spray so there was a huge amount of noise and dust. The holes were then charged with explosives and the floor was blasted. We then shovelled the redd up on to the face six feet above us and piled it up into 'roadside packs', pillars constructed from loose stones and dirt, which were used to support the roof where the coal had been stripped and the face conveyor moved over. These packs were about twenty feet long and were a bit like dry stone dykes. There were six of us, three trainees and three supervisors, and it generally took us two days to complete this task.

For refreshment we carried our drinking water in glass lemonade bottles and also tin flasks of sweet black tea wrapped in newspaper to try and keep some of its heat in. I usually filled mine just before leaving home at five-thirty in the morning and by ten o'clock it was lukewarm, but it shifted the dust from your throat and washed your piece down well.

A few shifts into our time at the training face, we found that someone was helping themselves to our water from our piece bags which we left hanging at the side of the tunnel. This was a rather nasty thing to do so we decided to teach whoever was responsible a lesson. I started to carry my water in a dark green beer bottle instead of the usual clear lemonade bottle, but the water kept disappearing so one day I decided to carry the light oil which we used to oil the workings of our puggers in this green bottle. As usual I left it in my piece bag when I went into the face to strip my stint and soon enough we could hear the retching of someone being very sick. It turned out to be one of the wood laddies from the loader. After being threatened with violence, the fireman made him drink some of it. It was a severe lesson for the lad to learn.

At the time I was doing my face training, Hamilton Town Hall was the venue of 'go as you please' contests where contestants from the audience performed in front of the dancers to win prizes. One

Monday morning, as we were waiting for the fireman, we discovered one of the trainees, a lad called Smithy, had won on the previous Saturday. Without too much persuasion we got him to give us a wee rendition, which he did in style on top of the main gate belt. Not to be outdone, one of the older supervisors performed the soft shoe shuffle on top of the belt. He was wearing knicky tams, an old cloth cap with a safety pin to hold his cap lamp (hard hats were not compulsory then), and didn't have a tooth in his head. He had us all falling about in fits.

It was while we were brushing the tail gate that I learned how to use explosives. The fireman taught me what to do: how to clean out the drillings and test for gas, prime the cartridge with the detonator and then put in the rest of the charge and stem it with clay, connect the detonators to the main shotfiring cable, post the sentries (a man stationed in a place of safety to prevent anyone from walking into the firing zone), and turn the key to set off the charges.

Myself and five other trainees brushed this tail gate on several occasions and we worked well together. The other trainees brushed the main gate which was bigger and required longer packs to be put in. They thought that we should all take turns doing the main gate brushing and we agreed to this, but during one of our turns in the tail gate we were teamed up with another supervisor whose trainee was a bit of a mouth and who nobody liked very much. I had had a couple of run-ins with him before, almost coming to blows, so there was no love lost between us.

For some reason he objected to me shotfiring the brushing and one time when I had posted the sentries, he sat on the brushing lip and refused to move. I coupled the detonator wires on to the shotfiring cable and told him to move, but again he refused. So I crawled down the face, gave the cable ends to my pal who took them and lay in tight to the coal face. I turned and, shining my light on to the exploder, I shouted "Fire!" and turned the key in the empty exploder. Well, he took off like a scalded cat, screaming at the top of his voice. When my supervisor saw what had happened he laid into me with a hawk shaft. In an eighteen inch high face I had no room to turn and nowhere to go, so I just had to lie there and take a right good hammering. But it was worth it because the trainee never bothered me again.

We also had another supervisor who came from the Highlands and when the belt was standing still for any length of time, he would sing softly in Gaelic. When it was all quiet on the face with everybody lying on their sides, this man and his lilting songs coming up the coal face was something to hear.

I finished my face training in January 1957 and left to be a spare faceman. I was still based at No.2 pit and I still had to do oncost work (i.e. any work except for face work) when there was no face work available. Since 1953 I had been going to Burnbank School of Engineering one day a week to study for my Ordinary National Certificate which I needed to become a mine manager. But like a lot of other young men my mind was on other things and I failed the course. However, I did make friends with three other lads while I was there, John from Blantyre, Bill from Kirkmuirhill and Davy from Larkhall. John was a clipper in Blantyre's Spittal pit and his father was the rope splicer. Bill was a drawer for a faceman in the Westoun Mine attached to Coalburn No.9, while Davy was a pony driver in the Quarter Mine on the banks of the River Avon. We were quite a versatile bunch.

We swapped stories about our pits and had many a laugh at the things that happened in them. Davy believed that pit ponies were very clever animals and he told us how they would know if an extra hutch had been attached to the rake they were pulling and would refuse to move until it was detached. He also said that his pit pony knew when it was finishing time. When the last rake was out at the foot of the surface mine, the pony would take off for the surface whenever he took its tail chains off. He was never able to keep up with it, so he would jump on its back and ride up to the surface. This was illegal and the manager would fine pony drivers if they were caught doing it (the money made from the fines was sent to the local hospital). The manager even posted one of his overmen at the surface to catch the drivers as they came out. One day as Davy came flying up he saw his dad, who was an overman, taking another driver's name and check numbers for riding his pony. Davy thought he would get let off, but his dad just looked up and took his name and numbers as well. There were no favourites there.

I heard a story from an old miner in Cardowan who told me of his younger days when he was a pony driver in the Ernoch pit in Burnbank. One day as he was taking his pony into a roadway it stopped and wouldn't go on. Suddenly he heard the scraping of rats and in the light of his carbide lamp saw a rats' flitting coming towards him. He climbed up the side of the roadway and held on to the supports as the rats passed underneath him. The mothers were carrying their young while others led the blind and lame with pieces of straw and bark off the props. The pony stood stock still while the rats were all around it, but they never touched it. After they had all passed the pony then went into the face workings. The old miner said that a few days later that same roadway collapsed, burying the miners working in there. They had unknowingly driven under an old shaft that had been filled with rubble. Due to the instability of the workings, rescue attempts were abandoned and the men's bodies had to be left buried underground.

During my time at Burnbank School we went on a couple of visits to other collieries. The first one was to Polkemmet Colliery at Whitburn to see a new type of power loader (a term applied to any power-operated machine for loading coal or any other material into mine cars, conveyors, road vehicles or bins). It was an adaptation of a coal cutting machine called the Samson Stripper. The coal face was pre-cut using an ordinary Samson chain machine. The stripper, which had a plough not unlike a half snow plough, would then be positioned at the side of the face and using hydraulic rams pushed up on to the roof for anchorage it would push into the cut coal, splitting it from the back of the undercut and pushing four feet of it at a time on to a chain conveyor. This never seemed to take off as a power loading machine and I never heard of it again, although it may have been used in other pits.

Our second visit was to the small Anderton mine situated in the moors above Glentaggart in Lanarkshire. There they used the stoop and room method which involved extracting coal in squares while leaving a pillar of coal in the middle to support the roof. The mine was so small that the manager also served as the fireman, engineer, electrician, and safety officer. He told us that when the mine was being sunk, he and his men had got down far enough to have the pithead gear built when the NCB abruptly decided to halt the work because the cost of building the surface gear was going to be too high. This would mean that the men would lose their jobs so the manager told the NCB that if they provided the steel work, he and his miners would build their own pithead. The NCB consented and the work went ahead.

The miners in this mine drilled their shot holes and charged them with black gunpowder, using a fuse known as a strum to fire them. The strum had to be lit with the naked flame of their carbide lamps. They excavated sections twelve feet wide by six high and they earned about five pounds a shift for what was very hard and dangerous work. There were no pit baths and at the end of their shifts they had to travel home in their wet and dirty pit clothes.

Six

Cardowan, 1957 - 1958

As I knew how to use lashing chains, I was sent to the Main East haulage road to send the rakes of hutches into the loader. This road was at the foot of the tunnel where I used to push the hutches to when I first went underground. I was paid twenty-four shillings and eleven pence a shift. I worked five shifts a week and was paid a bonus shift (i.e. if I worked all five I was paid the money for a sixth as well), but if I missed just one shift then I would lose the bonus shift as well. I also worked every second Saturday, six until twelve, but thanks to the pithead baths at least I was able to go out on a Saturday afternoon straight from the pit. There was also the occasional Sunday shift.

In the Main East I worked with three other lads and we all had nicknames: mine was Terry and I was joined by Bugs Bunny, Squib Mcguigan and J.J. Our under manager was called Willie Hill and he was a great guy. One day Bugs, who was a natural artist and could make anything out of clay, made a lifesize bust of J.J. We put it on a set of poles and dressed it in oilskins and put J.J.'s helmet and lamp on it. Then we sat it in a dark recess just inside the steel ventilation doors. First through was Willie, who said "Morning J.J." and when he got no reply he asked him if he was sleeping. On closer inspection he saw it was only a dummy and what he called us is unrepeatable.

One of the tasks I got as a spare faceman was to carry girders into the face for the brushers. At the Main East girder carriers were on contract and were paid according to the size and number of girders they took into the face. These were called arch girders and consisted of two separate halves to make a complete arch. There were three sizes: seven feet by seven feet, ten feet by eight, and twelve feet by nine. My task was to take them from the main tunnel into the main gate and the tail gate. I would load the twelve by nines on to a bogie and push it to the end of the rails in the main gate, off-loading them to the side. Taking a half-arch on my shoulder, I would then carry it over the very rough and uneven tunnel floor to the face which was about two hundred yards or more in. There they were placed at the side of the road for the brushers. The main gate was the easiest to get into, for when you went into the tail gate you had to drag the ten by eight girder through a set of air doors into the roadway. If I was lucky the road had not crushed down and I would have enough standing room to load the girders on to a bogie (the pressure exerted by the roof 'crushing down' on to the girders caused them to bend and the timber around them to break, meaning that the height between the road and the roof would become increasingly low). If the roadway had crushed down I had to drag the girders through by hand until I reached a place where I could get it on to my shoulder and carry it into the face. This was what happened most times.

It was very difficult balancing these girders on your shoulder as they were five inches and four inches broad respectively. They were also an awkward shape as one end was rounded and the other was a straight leg so the centre was hard to find. When I thought I had the right balance and was on my way they would start to twist and slew making a nightmare of moving them. My shoulders ended up sore and skinned even though I tried to protect them by placing a bag between them and the girder. The rate for the job averaged out at about seventy shillings a shift.

One day the winding engine blew a piston and we were stuck underground. Some of the miners were sent to get up No.1 shaft. This involved going to the bottom level at No.2 which was 240 feet below No.1 and getting on an emergency cage which was attached to the bottom of the main cage by a steel winding rope. The cage was then pulled up to No.1 pit bottom and the men were transferred to the main cage to ascend to the surface. It was a pretty hairy operation as there was no guide ropes on the emergency cage and it turned and twisted on its way up.

The rest of the men, including myself, waited at the bottom of No.2 to get the cage up this shaft. When the cage arrived, there was a shaftsman on it. He allowed only ten men on the cage, along with himself. He got us on to the cage and told us to hang on while the cage took off at material speed (the winder had two speeds: one for men and the other for material which was faster). It left the bottom and travelled up about thirty feet before crashing down again. Once more it took off and once more it came down again. At the third attempt it got away and sped up the shaft. My knuckles went white as I hung on like grim death while the cage hurtled up, not slowing in mid-shaft and rattling and shaking because it was only working on one cylinder. I don't know which was worse, No.1 emergency cage or riding this bucking bronco, but we got to the surface in the end.

During this time I was also stripping coal wherever I was needed. It was around this time that power loading was introduced to Cardowan. In the Main East side a new face had been developed which was only two feet high. To work it we used the plough, a system developed in Germany which consisted of a metal box with cutting tools at one end. It was pulled up and down the face by steel ropes which were operated by two haulage engines at either end. The plough removed the coal on the bottom half of the face and we had to knock the tops down with our puggers. The plough could only remove about four inches with every cut and the coal was loaded on to steel chain conveyor pans called panzers. They were made in Germany and were of solid steel just like a tank. After about eighteen inches had been stripped off, the pans were pushed over using hand ratchets and then we pugged the tops down. It was awkward work, very dusty, and splinters would hit my eyes which ended up all red and sore.

At each end of the face there was a section called a stable hole, which was hand stripped to allow the plough access to the rest of the face. At the top end stable the rope for drawing the plough up went round a pulley wheel and out the tail gate to the haulage engine. This pulley wheel was anchored to the roof by wooden props, known as stells, which were set at an angle to prevent movement. This was where I first encountered a fatal accident. As the plough was being flitted back up the face it snagged and the force of the powerful haulage caused the wooden props to break, causing the rope and the pulley wheel to crash into the side of the steel conveyor. Unfortunately a stripper called Bladdie Wilson was working between the rope and the conveyor when the wheel came away and he was crushed against the conveyor. The roof collapsed and the rest of the strippers got off the face as quickly as they could, except Bladdie's mate. He crawled over to where Bladdie was lying and tried to pull the rope off him. He was shouting to the others to come back and help him and when they did get back they found that Bladdie had been killed outright. Bladdie was a Lithuanian and where I lived in Glasgow there was a Lithuanian family called Wilson. Mrs Wilson used to ask me if I ever met her brother-in-law who worked in Cardowan. Because of her broken English, I always thought she called him Billie but I discovered that Bladdie was in fact her relative. I was a very sad miner when I went home to the street that night.

I had a few shifts in that same stable during my time as a spare stripper and the stripper in charge was Bladdie's mate, Shorty. He was one of the hard men of Cardowan village. He would fight anybody at the drop of a hat so you can imagine how I felt, a green stripper, going into work with him. I found that if I asked him what he wanted me to do - for example, should I pug or shovel? - he would say that I was to do whatever I wanted to do; but if I told him what I was going to do, say the shovelling, he would tell me to do the pugging.

Later on, after the new plough section went into full production there were difficulties in pugging down the top six inches of coal that was left on by the plough. So a night shift was introduced and Shorty was put in charge. At the same time Overtoun Mains Colliery flooded and some of its miners were transferred to Cardowan. Some of the Overtoun strippers were put into the plough section on the dayshift going turn about with Shorty's crew and one of them called Crawford, nicknamed Craw, would chalk messages on a shovel, telling Shorty and his crew what a lazy shower they were and to get their fingers out and work harder. I was in this group and some of us warned him about Shorty's temper and told him he would be better off not leaving messages like that. "I'm not afraid of Shorty. I'll sort him out if he tries anything," was Craw's reply.

One morning soon after this I was walking along with the other strippers towards the pithead doors, when suddenly they burst open and out came Shorty and his crew. They should have left the section and been up the pit half an hour ago. "Where's this bastard called Craw?" Shorty roared, staring into everyone's faces.

"I am," said Craw, stepping forward, chest out like a hard man, "so what?" Then Shorty hit him square in the jaw, the blow coming with all the hate the man could muster. His fist was like a piston from the steam winder and down Craw went, flat on his back, eyes glazed. "Get up and fight like a man," Shorty roared at him and I was half expecting him to pick Craw up and belt him again, but there was no movement from Craw at all. We went over to Shorty and got him away before any of the gaffers came or he would have been in serious trouble. Craw was helped up and taken underground by his mates. There were no more messages left after that, in fact Craw and his crew went back to Overtoun Mains soon afterwards when the pit was pumped out.

After working on the plough section I was sent to No.2 east section, a two foot seam where the coal was very hard to strip. I was sent to a place just up from the main gate where I worked beside an old Lithuanian miner who wore a cloth cap instead of a helmet. I found that the coal here just would not give and I couldn't even 'cut in' to the face (i.e. excavate a section of coal face four feet by five feet which allowed the pressure of the roof to burst out the coal). It was about piece time and I still hadn't got started so up came the old chap and in broken English he asked if I would watch what he was going to show me. I said I would and he placed my pugger against the coal, showing me the natural cleat, and started to pug into this, gradually enlarging away from it. Cutting at an angle, using the cleat as a guiding plane, he soon had me well on my way. He helped me until my place was about stripped before he returned to his own place. They hadn't taught us how to strip this kind of coal at the training face, but it seemed that many of the old strippers had a few tricks up their sleeves.

When I was not on the face or on oncost, I was sent to work with the gas drainage crew. Work had already begun to extract firedamp from the strata above and below the coal faces. The reason for this was that one day the government inspector had been making an inspection of a faceline that had recently gone into production and he decided to take a gas test at the fifth air split from the face. (A split was a small section left open in the brushing pack to allow air to travel up the face to the tail gate; there was one placed about every twenty-five yards as the face advanced). He lowered his lamp to the testing flame and put it into the split. The gas exploded inside his lamp (which had two internal gauzes which only allowed gas to ignite within the lamp and not spread outside) and this meant there was more than five percent of firedamp present. He went to the next split and tested it with the undermanager's lamp, and again it exploded. The undermanager was already beginning to have kittens. Moving on to split number three, he gently put the fireman's lamp in it and this time the testing flame of the lamp indicated a very high reading. He was going to close the section there and then and they immediately went to the surface, but the next thing we heard was that there was to be a gas drainage programme.

This involved laying a twenty-four inch wide pipeline from the surface and into the sections in the east and west sides of the pit. We had to work many an extra shift as well as weekend work to install them and once they were in position, the gas drainage began. We would bore into the roof for six feet, then install a stand pipe which had a flexible clamp with a hose attached. A narrower drill was then driven up through this stand pipe and drilled up to a height of 150 feet or until gas was struck. The drill would be withdrawn and the flexible clamp bolted on to the stand pipe and the hose attached to the twenty-four inch steel main pipe. The gas was then pumped to the pithead and was used to fire the steam boilers.

At one point as we were drilling we struck thick crude oil, as well as water, and then a large discharge of gas. Then, to crown everything, the blasted drill got stuck so we had to struggle to free it while getting covered in oil and having the gas drainage officer playing compressed air over us in an attempt to prevent us from being overcome by gas. Doing that the idiot might have sparked off an explosion, but we eventually got everything under control and connected the flexible hose.

A sample of this oil was sent to the labs and it was reckoned that it would cost £100 to produce one gallon of petrol from it. The problem was how to separate it from the gas, but some engineer came up with a solution and it was very simple. Bell-end pieces were inserted into the main gas pipe between its couplings and the ends of these were placed inside ordinary buckets filled with oil. Being heavier than the gas, when the crude oil flowed down the main pipe it would drop down the bell-end and into the pail, and then overflow on to the floor of the roadway. This road was used only by the top end strippers and the wood laddies, and as the overflow of oil was not very heavy it did not present too much of a problem. However, once as some of the strippers were going by the overflow into the face one of them lost his balance and landed flat on his back and was covered in oil. He just picked himself up and continued into the face and stripped his place then went up the pit. The face line stank of oil and sweat for days after.

The methods we used to extract the gas and pipe it to the surface were modern and moderately safe. In the nineteenth century the Victoria pit in West Wemyss, Fife, suffered from a similar problem and the only way it could be dealt with at that time was by drilling boreholes in the roof of the coal and igniting the gas at the mouth of these holes. This was obviously very dangerous. The same year gas started to be piped to the surface at my pit, there was a disastrous explosion at Kames Colliery in Ayrshire when an emission of gas from a borehole was ignited accidentally. It was a naked light mine and the explosion caused the death of several miners.

Eventually, No.2 East reached its allowed distance, approaching the area below Gartloch hospital. We were unable to mine the coal in this area as the NCB had to leave a pillar of coal and the seam went up from eighteen inches to three feet or more in height. On the last shift of No.2 East we went on to the face and instead of taking a full strip off all we did was lift the loose coal lying around, gather up our tools and go to the main gate for piece time. We had a sing-song and a 'go as you please' before going up the pit at two o'clock.

On the Tuesday of the following week we got our pool line (the strip of paper indicating the amount of money you had earned each day). It showed us that between Monday and Thursday we were getting between seventy-five and eighty shillings per day, but on Friday we only got ten. The pool leader went in to see the under-manager, Willie Hill, and pointed out that the least he could pay us for Friday was thirty-four shillings for the work we had done. In reply to this Willie said, "You all had a party down my pit, didn't you?".

"Yes, but -"

"No buts - you did and you didn't invite me!" whereupon he went into his desk drawer and brought out another pool line giving us all seventy shillings for Friday. He wasn't a bad sport - I can't see any manager doing that today.

Eventually I got my own regular place in the new plough section. The stripper who worked next to me was called Pat and he weighed around fifteen stone. On the day he started he had to go to his old section and get his tool but on the way back he slipped on the steel plates at the loader and twisted his back. Nevertheless, he did his stint and at piece time came off the face to have his piece. However, when he tried to get up to go back to work he found he couldn't move. We all tried to pull him up but it was no good so we sent for the fireman who organised a stretcher to carry Pat out of the pit. At the surface the nurse sent him to hospital in an ambulance and me and another miner called Tommy went along with him.

At the hospital Pat was put on a trolley. The nurse didn't even cover him with a blanket and as he was only wearing a peewit and moleskin trousers it wasn't long before he was shivering with cold. After an hour or more he still hadn't been attended to so Tommy went to see what was going on. He returned with a doctor who simply got a nurse to give Pat a blanket before disappearing again. We were astounded, but undaunted Tommy went off again and this time succeeded in getting Pat X-rayed. After Pat returned he lay for another long time until a doctor came along and gave him the news about his injuries. There was nothing broken - he had only twisted a muscle in his back so he was being sent home. All this time, Pat hadn't been able to wash himself or change out of his smelly pit clothes and he had to go home just as filthy as he was when he was taken out of the pit. Once home, he couldn't even get into the bath to wash himself and his wife had to call a neighbour in to help her wash him. Poor guy, he was totally embarrassed. Even in 1957 it seemed that some people still considered miners to be second-class.

My place at the coal face was next to the top corner that ran along the side of the waste of a section that had been excavated. The roof here was often broken and extra supports had to be put in. The area of roof over me was particularly bad and as the wood laddie went up to my mate's place with his supports, I asked him to leave me a strap along with my props. As soon as I had stripped out enough coal I set my props in and the strap between them (like goalposts) and then I continued to strip the rest of my stint.

I was up at the waste end when the roof started to cave in. The props were splitting, pieces of stone were falling on me and the noise was terrible. It was like an express train going over a steel bridge. I tried to crawl out on my belly but the stones of the roof started to fall on my ankles, then on to my legs and then I was stuck! The falling stones and debris continued up my legs, on to my buttocks, rising on to my back. I was in sheer panic. My face was pressed down on to the floor and my hands were cut and bleeding from trying to pull myself out. The middle of the strap was broken and jagged and it cut into me as it took the weight. Then everything stopped - the strap was holding and the debris stopped falling. The splintered wood of the strap was cutting into my neck, but I felt that my guardian angel had saved me once again. Eventually the other miners dug me free and I went out to the tail gate, sat down and had a drink of cold sweet tea. It tasted better than anything I had ever tasted before. I don't mind saying that I gave a little prayer while I sat there.

After a while I decided to go to the pit bottom to get up the pit. Tommy came to see how I was doing, and seeing that I was about to leave he asked, "What about your mate?".

I said, "There are plenty of strippers to dig for him. They don't need me - I'm off."

"No you're not." he said and when I went to push past him, he hit me square on the chin, knocking me flat on my back. "Now back in you go, or you'll get another one."

I didn't argue and back in I went. He said to me later that if I hadn't gone back into the face, I might never have gone back. The whole experience had been pretty scary. When I did go up the face there were still some trickles from the roof and every time this happened, I was on the move. When we did get to my mate he was surrounded by props. There were more trees in there than in Epping Forest. All this for thirty-four shillings and eleven pence a shift, plus six and tuppence and three farthings a ton.

I had a mate who after his face training went to be a stripper in No.1 pit. He was digging away one day when the roof collapsed on top of him. He was completely buried and when they got his face cleared he was hardly breathing and was totally still. He couldn't even speak. They thought he was dying and as he was a Catholic, they sent for a priest. The face was only eighteen inches high but the priest gave my mate his last rites and eventually they got him out. They carried him out to the pit bottom where he lay stock still on the stretcher, hardly breathing and not moving, but when they got him to the surface and into the medical room, he started to move his hands, then his arms and then everything came back. He had been absolutely terrified and had suffered a form of paralysis. Later, once he had recovered from his wounds he went back to the stripping, but it took him a while to forget what had happened. He used to joke about being the only miner in the pit to have had his last rites in advance.

During 1957 I went to Burnbank School one night a week for a ten week course to get my shotfirer qualification. I also went to Coatbridge Tech and sat my gas testing and hearing test. During the test I had to determine the amount of firedamp that was present inside five flame safety lamps. There were small cones of blue burning above the flame in three of them. A very small cone represented one and a quarter percent firedamp in the air which meant that all electrical equipment in a section should be switched off and all shotfiring stopped. A cone shaped like a triangle represented two and a half percent which required the withdrawal of men from a section. A long thin cone reaching up inside the lamp represented the start of the explosive range which went from five up to fourteen percent, with the most violent explosion being at nine percent when the mixture of oxygen and firedamp would be at its most explosive.

If gas ignites in a pit there is usually an initial explosion which also ignites all the coal dust lying about in a tunnel and travels inwards. After this the air pressure builds up and this may cause a return explosion which ignites any coal dust that may be left. The gas that is left is called 'afterdamp' and if by that point the explosions haven't got you then the gas will as there is no oxygen left at all. It has been known for a large haulage machine to have been ripped from its seating and blown into a tunnel for more than a hundred yards in an initial explosion and then, on the return explosion, being brought back near to its original position.

By this time I was also engaged to a girl called Margo who was a singer in a band and on the trades holiday the following year we went to Montrose for a break. I think half of Cardowan was there as well. A lot of the miners camped on the green where they were entertained by Frankie Jones and Walter McGowan, two well-known boxers who put on exhibitions for the public. One night we all met in the Harbour Bar for a sing-song. There was this guy who worked in No.1 pit called Casey who looked real tough and had a nose that must have been broken a few times. Well, he got up to sing an opera song called 'Catarie' and he was absolutely brilliant. Over the years I've heard a few famous singers perform that song but I still think Casey gave one of the best renditions I've ever heard.

One Sunday we went to Kirkcaldy to see Margo's relations. We got off the train and caught the bus to take us to the area where Margo's aunt stayed. The bus was an ancient make called a Guy and when we boarded it we got a shock - it was 1958 and here was a bus that still had wooden seats. The conductress wasn't very pleased when I asked her if Fife knew that the war had ended in 1945.

Margo's cousin Margaret worked for the NCB at their area headquarters. She showed me a glossy handbook about the new Rothes Colliery at Thornton. The pit was described in glowing terms and the book also promised housing for the miners in the new town of Glenrothes. "That's for me," I said. So I went back to Cardowan and applied for a transfer.

Seven
Rothes, 1958

In June 1958 I found myself standing in front of the twin towers of Rothes Colliery, part of a crowd waiting to see the Queen and Prince Philip who were touring the coal faces. I think it was the first time Her Majesty had been underground and she visited a face called the Five Foot Lateral while the Prince went to the Five Foot at No.1 South. The Prince apparently took a miners pick and pulled a lump of coal off the face. "How much do I get for that?" he asked the stripper.

"Well sir," the stripper replied, pointing to two chalk marks on the roof, "see that chalk mark there and the other one down there?"

"Yes?"

"Well, if you strip all the coal between them and four and a half feet in you will be paid £2 and 12 shillings."

The stripper was actually told off for saying that to the Prince.

I saw the royal couple leave and I was then allowed into the colliery and went to meet the manager, Tommy Barrie, who signed me on and told me to report to Matthew Peden, the undermanager, in the morning. I then went and arranged to get lockers in the baths and went to the check office for my checks. There were three in total: a round one that you kept on you, an oblong one that you put in a slot when you took out your lamp, and a square one that you gave to the banksman (whose job was to load and unload the cage at the top of the shaft) before you went underground.

Everything was enclosed at this pit including the winding wheels in the towers, the baths and the entrance to the car hall where the mine cars, large hutches holding three tons of material, were shunted from the cage and emptied and then returned to the cage. At the entrance to the car hall there was a notice marking it as a 'No Naked Light' area where no cigarettes or matches were allowed. There was a wooden hut here where a fireman or deputy kept watch. His job was to choose a miner at random who was taken into the hut where he was searched for contraband by another deputy while a third was present as a witness in case any was found. I thought this was a bit strange because in Cardowan we would never ever have taken any contraband underground. Because the pit was so gassy, everyone trusted each other.

I got digs with Mrs Moss in Dura Crescent in Woodside (only Woodside and Auchmuty precincts had so far been built in Glenrothes). There were two other Rothes miners staying there and Mrs Moss's only stipulation was that she would not be responsible for getting us up, but would leave the table set for our breakfast and have our pieces made up. The pits in Fife started at six o'clock rather than seven as they did in the west. This meant getting up at four, having breakfast, and catching a pit bus at ten past five.

On my first morning I went along to the shaft quite early to have a look around. The shaft had four cages in it: two had single decks and went down to 333 fathoms (1,998 feet), and the other two had four decks, each of which could hold a three ton mine car, and these went down to a level of 266 fathoms (always referred to as the 1,600 feet level). The cages were driven by two winding engines that sat in a tower, two hundred feet tall, directly above the shaft. Known as Koepe Winders, they were of a German design and electrically driven. A continental system of winding coal to the surface, a comparatively light friction pulley was used instead of a heavy drum, thereby cutting power costs considerably. Over the pulley an endless rope passed and the cages or skips were attached to this. When the cages with the mine cars arrived at the surface the banksman, from inside a cabin, operated rams that pushed the empty car on to the cage. This would dislodge the full one which would run down an incline and, using a system of retarders, would go into a tumbler and be emptied on to a belt, taking the coal to the washer straight away. This system made picking tables a thing of the past (thank goodness). This was continued until all four decks had been dealt with. When the mine car left the tumbler it ran down a slope, then up an incline over spring switches. Bouncing off a spring buffer it then went down on to a creeper that took it back round to the front of the shaft to start all over again. All of this took place under cover.

I arrived at the cages and gave my square check to the banksman and went on to the cage. The first thing I noticed was a canopy inside the cage and I wondered what it was for, but as we hurtled downwards I saw that the sides of the shaft were running with water and I realised that the canopies were to keep the miners dry as they went underground. During the sinking of the shafts which started in 1948, there were problems with flooding and by 1950 it was reported that the inflow of water into the shaft was about one hundred gallons per minute. However, the sinking of the shafts continued, albeit at a very slow rate. In 1955 a massive intrusion of water from a couple of boreholes - three hundred gallons per minute - flooded the shaft. The *Daily Record* reported that No.1 shaft was flooded to a depth of ninety feet. A diver was brought in to try and plug the holes but it was too dangerous for him, so heavier pumping equipment was used. No.1 shaft reached its final depth of 418 fathoms in 1956, seven and a half years after the work began. During sinking various methods had been used to control the water and as a result pipes were left sticking out of the side of the shaft with water pouring out of them, thus the use of canopies.

I got off at the 1,600 feet level and went round to a pump house where Matthew Peden had his office. The first question he asked me was, "Where are your tools?" I was puzzled and asked what he meant. At this I thought he was going to have a fit. "Your shovel, pick, etc." he said. This was lesson No.1.

"I haven't any."

"Why not?"

"Well, where I come from you just used the tools of the man whose place you were going to strip."

"Bloody West Coasters," he said. "In this pit you carry your tools about with you on a bar called a speke which has a padlock on it."

Full of trust weren't they. He told me to get tools for the next day or I wouldn't be able to be a face worker at this pit. In the meantime I was put on oncost and sent into the Lochgelly Splint section to clean up between the rails at the loader.

Lesson No.2 came just as I arrived at the Splint. This six foot, obnoxious giant - who will remain nameless - came out ranting and raving at me like a lunatic for not having tools. How could I clean up his section? With my bare hands? He was going on and on and I just about lost my job before I'd even got started. I had never encountered an idiot like this before and was on the point of telling him so when a local miner who had also been sent in to clean up intervened. "He can use my spare tools," he said, whereupon the raving lunatic calmed down a bit and went off. "Don't mind him," I was told, "He used to be the pit bottom rope splicer in one of the local pits and the position of overman has gone to his head." I never got on with that overman all the time I worked in Rothes.

On getting to the surface that day I went right to the stores and purchased the necessary tools and the bar to carry them on. Next day I reported once more to Peden and I was sent to see the over-man in the Five Foot sections. I was told to strip in a section named No.1 Slope. This face went uphill for a good distance and when I got there I got a bit of a shock. Standing in the main gate, the left hand side of the face had five feet of coal and two feet of slate like stone - called 'blae' - on top, making it seven feet in height. On the right hand side there was barely three feet of coal with a fairly solid roof. I reported to the deputy who told me to go up to the left hand corner and strip it - "See Pete and he'll show you your marks." I went up to the corner and the stripper showed me my marks. It was only about two yards.

"Not very long," I said.

"Long enough," he replied.

Well, I started to shovel away the gum (the cuttings from the coal cutter as it undercuts the face) then put some wedges into the undercut to prevent the coal from falling over on me. Lesson No.3: after I had lifted all the gum the hole borer came up and bored two holes in my place.

"How do I fire my place?" I inquired.

"Don't know," said the hole borer and away he went.

There I was, place ready, but no explosives to fire it. The face was enormous - what a difference from eighteen inches high. Fortunately, Pete had a tin ammunition box which was apparently how you carried your explosives down the pit. He carried ten pounds of explosives and generally two or more strippers, depending on how much they needed, shared a box and took turns carrying it down each day. The shotfirer was able to use some of Pete's stuff to blow down my coal and after it was fired I shovelled enough away to be able to set some supports.

Lesson No.4 was how to get a seven feet steel strap up to the roof and hammer up a seven feet wooden prop. The answer was co-operation. I held Pete's strap and he hammered up his props, and then he held my strap and I hammered up my props. We continued like that until the place was stripped.

The next day I was sent back into the Lochgelly Splint, my favourite overman's section. I was to help the stripper in a place just below the main gate. The coal was faulted there and the place was actually a sump full of water. I didn't have oilskins so I got soaked. The deputy said he would give me a line to let me up the pit half an hour early - big deal! The face was only about two feet six inches high and there was a compressed air pump going beside me all through the shift. I wondered what had happened to the so-called power loading. I had left a dry, gassy, warm pit, earning eighty shillings a shift, to land in this wet, miserable hole for the princely sum of fifty-two shillings. Here I was, up to my armpits in muck and water with a raving loony as a gaffer - I must have flipped to have taken the job.

Over the next three days I worked in the same place. I was going daft and the overman definitely had it in for me. I asked for oilskins and he told me there were none. "Well, I'm not going in there without them," I replied. He just about had a heart attack, if he had a heart, that is. "If you don't get in there I'll send you up the pit and cut your pay," he roared.

"Try it and see what happens."

I would have gone to somebody higher up about this idiot, but he sent me away to a waste drivage to work. I was there for a day or two and then was sent to the Five Foot, a marked rebel.

I was spare face worker for this area and did some stripping, brushing, and anything else that was required of me. There was another spare face worker called Willie Herd who was sent to No.1 Slope to shovel the gum along the side of the face pans. He started at one end and kept shovelling until he reached the other end. He then discovered that the coal cutter had only cut a twelve inch undercut (the usual was four and a half feet) to give the strippers a 'flyer' (a quick shift) before their annual holidays. Willie had unwittingly stripped the whole run and when they found out what he had done, the strippers in that section demanded that their union should get him sacked. Willie's mistake had done them out of an easy shift for full stripping wages and as a result they were sent to other more difficult sections to work on their last shift. How petty could they get? Anyway, the manager wouldn't accept this and told them so.

The pit stopped for the trade holidays and I went off to Scarborough for two weeks. When I got back I started back on the stripping at No.1 South and Willie was sent to the No.1 Slope where the strippers refused to work with him and they all came off the face, refusing to go back on until he was sent somewhere else. This happened a few times but the management refused to be blackmailed by them, telling them that if they came off again their time would be stopped until they went back on. This caused a brief strike, but eventually things settled down and got back to normal.

Meanwhile, two new lodgers arrived at our digs. They came from Germany and were trainee mine managers who had been sent to Rothes to gain experience of mining in Scotland. One was called Karl Heinz Reumer and the other was called Gunther Swallow. They told us what it was like in the German coal industry. Apparently, at college they wore uniforms like navy officers. They stayed with us for a couple of months before returning to Germany. When I was getting married I got a card from Gunther, wishing us well.

I was sent to No.1 Slope North to strip and was given a place halfway down. I had to strip fourteen yards of coal three feet high with a four feet six inch undercut which worked out at about fourteen tons of coal, roughly a ton per yard at this height, for fifty-two shillings a shift. It looked like a very long way to strip - from my starting chalk mark, I couldn't see the end one.

It was now August and I was getting into the swing of things. One morning, as I was lifting the gum the deputy shouted up the run for me. Puzzled, I went down to the main gate where he asked me if I had a shotfiring certificate. I said I did and he told me to go and see the deputy on No.1 South. This deputy gave me a flame safety lamp, a bag containing forty detonators, a length of shotfiring cable, a cleaner, a stemmer, an exploder and key to operate it. "Off you go then," he told me, "the strippers are waiting for you."

It was a very nervous twenty-one year old who went on to the face at No.1 South, although the strippers turned out to be very helpful. I soon learned the right amount of explosives to put in the hole and to send a stripper up the face in the opposite direction from myself to be the sentry (who stood at the entry to the danger zone during shotfiring to prevent anyone from entering until all the shots had been fired). I would then connect the detonator wires to the shot-firing cable and, taking up a safe position, would connect it to the exploder, shout a warning and insert the key and turn it, exploding the charge. After firing I would go into the area and test for gas to ensure the place was safe for the men to return to.

It was on this face a little while later that I had my one and only shotfiring accident. I had prepared two shots in the coal and had sent the stripper up the run as the sentry. After connecting the shotfiring cable to my six shot exploder, the circuit light came on letting me know everything was in order. I shouted my warning and exploded the two charges, but as I was waiting for the reek and dust to clear a figure came staggering out of it and collapsed in my arms. His front was covered in blood and I thought, "My God, I've killed him." Gently, I laid him down and shouted for help. The other strippers arrived fairly quickly and helped me to examine him. I was looking at his front trying to ascertain the seriousness of his injuries and to my relief I discovered that the blood was coming from punctures in his arms and that he had no life-threatening internal injuries. Lumps of coal were embedded in his arms, as if they had been fired from a shotgun. The deputy and a first aid man arrived and I found out the miner was Willie Herd.

I went up the run to the sentries, asking what had happened. They had obviously let Willie through, but denied even seeing him. I told them that they couldn't have missed him as he must have come right between them. It turned out that they had been talking about football, so they said, although remembering Herd's trouble with the strippers, some people had their doubts. Willie was taken to the surface on a stretcher and then on to hospital. He never came back to Rothes and I later heard that he emigrated to Canada.

I went up the pit that day a very worried man and I was summoned to the office of the general manager, Mr Forthringham, to give my report on the incident. Mr Forthringham and Mr Barrie were there along with the pit safety officer and a policeman. They put me through the third degree with an awful lot of questions which I was able to answer satisfactorily. I was told to return to my shotfiring duties the next day, although a lot of the deputies and shotfirers had been convinced that I would be suspended until an enquiry had been carried out.

Next day, as I was shotfiring on the run, I was sent to meet the government inspector who had the power to sack or demote anyone who had not adhered to the Coal Mines Act. He asked me to repeat what had happened on the face the previous day and as I spoke to him he ran his walking stick along the coal coming out on the conveyor belt. I wondered if he was even listening to me, had he already made up his mind? Eventually, when I stopped, he asked me two questions: why was I firing two shots and what kind of exploder was I using? I told him the reason for firing two shots was to allow the stripper to set his supports. The shots were placed one above the other and allowed the head coal to come down along with the main coal. This would have allowed the steel strap to clean the roof. The type of exploder I was using was a six shot exploder.

"Well, lad," he said, "Everything you did was in order and I can't fault you, but in future look up the face before you set off your charges as you might see someone coming down the run."

The miner who had been the sentry was charged by the police and tried at Kirkcaldy Sheriff Court. He was found guilty and fined fourteen pounds, a weeks wages to him.

After a spell in the Five Foot, I was sent once more to work beside my favourite overman in the Lochgelly Splint, where the face was going through some very faulted ground. The face pans were known as shaking or jigging pans as they moved up and down like the shakers at the tables. Each pan was thirteen feet long and moved along the whole length of the face. The coal was shunted down to the main gate loader by the up and down movement and it was surprising how much coal was shifted by this method. I was sent in to fire the fault on the backshift. When I got there the strippers had it all bored and gave me the explosives can. When I opened it the type of explosive was different to the type I was used to. It was called Polar Ajax. I asked them what was the difference and they said there was none, it was just the same. Here was Lesson No.5: don't trust the buggers.

I stemmed up the holes using the same amount as normal, crawled up the face and fired the charges. By the amount of noise and reek, I realised something wasn't right. When I went down to inspect the area I had fired I found coal and stone every where and the jigging pan twisted right round like a corkscrew, all bent and buckled. Fortunately, the deputy on this shift was not like my raving loony of an overman and asked what had happened. I told him about the Polar Ajax and he told me that this was a tunnel explosive and shouldn't have been used in coal. He got on to the strippers - they should not have received that type of explosive and he was going to see the magazine man to find out why he had given it to them. He then told them to get the pan replaced and clean up the mess and told me to go and help the other shotfirers.

It was on this fault that I came to know some of the other chaps who had come out from the west. One man, Pat, had a little boy who was suffering from a rupture but was too young to have an operation. One day during his piece time Pat fell asleep and was found by my favourite overman along with Mr Barrie, the manager. When the overman saw Pat he started ranting and raving and actually kicked Pat awake. Roaring at the top of his voice, he told Pat that he was sacked. "Get away up the pit! You'll also be charged by the police." However, Mr Barrie told the overman to shut up and that he would deal with the situation. The overman was sent into the face and Mr Barrie sat down beside Pat. He asked him if everything was all right and if there was anything wrong, so Pat told him about his son, the constant pain the wee fellow was in, and how his wife was at the end of her tether. Pat was trying to do everything he could to help, even walking the floor with the boy during the night and not getting any sleep as a result. Mr Barrie asked how long it would be before the lad would get his operation. Pat said three months so Mr Barrie offered him a spell on the backshift, starting the next day. My favourite overman's gas was certainly put at a peep. Some people said Mr Barrie didn't have a heart, but they were wrong - this time anyway.

Eight
Rothes, 1959

In March 1959 I got married to Margo in a little church on the South Side of Glasgow, and that month I was also sent to work in the pit bottom area to organise the transporting of materials and empties into the sections and getting the full cars of coal out to the pit bottom.

This job gave me my introduction to electric locomotives. There were two types: one was a Metro Vickers, maximum speed twenty miles per hour, which had a cabin at each end so it could be easily driven in opposite directions without turning; the other, known as a 'Green Bat', had only one driving position and could reach a speed of about ten miles per hour.

With these machines going to and fro the men had to be careful when walking in the tunnels and they were only allowed on to the tunnel roads at certain times of the shift. The full cars of coal and redd were brought to a siding on the south side of the pit, then shunted into the tracks towards the shaft. They were pushed into the pit bottom and up to the cages by means of rams and retarders. The onsetter, who was responsible for pushing the cars on to the cages, sat up in a cabin similar to the one on the surface and using rams he would push the full car on to a deck of the cage, dislodging an empty which would run out on to tracks to be coupled into twenty-five-car trains which were taken into the sections by the electric locomotives.

My job was to try and keep things moving and do any troubleshooting that might be required. I had to work with this deputy - who I'll call Jack - who delighted in contradicting any order I gave whenever he could (being the deputy he had more say than I had). For example, I would tell a driver to take a train of empties into the Lochgelly Splint and bring out the full cars. Meanwhile, Jack would get a phone call from the Cardenden section looking for some timber or girders, and finding maybe two cars of supplies in the pit bottom for that section he would tell the loco driver to take them into the Cardenden instead of going to the Lochgelly. As a result the Lochgelly would run out of empties and have a surplus of full cars waiting to be hauled to the pit bottom. The deputy in the Lochgelly would then phone the pump house as this was the contact point and to crown everything the old pumper couldn't wait to report this to Matt Peden, who in turn would get on to yours truly. This happened on numerous occasions and I was getting fed up with it. I told Jack and Sneaky the old pumper to lay off or I'd blow my top and they wouldn't like it. Things settled down for a while but Jack couldn't leave it alone and soon started his old tricks again. I found I was chasing my tail once more so I told Matt Peden to put me back on the shotfiring. I think he was glad to do so because the aggro was getting too much.

I was sent to work with the Cementation Company (which was subcontracted by the NCB to make large tunnels through rock) in the South Lateral Mine which was being driven from the south side of the pit to reach the Lochgelly Splint. It was a locomotive road about eighteen feet high and twenty feet wide. There was a tunnelling crew of six men called drifters and the work was supervised by a Cementation Company supervisor and NCB officials of the Rothes pit who were legally responsible for any contracted workman underground in their pit.

The tunnel face had around ninety holes bored in it and using about two hundred pounds of explosives with half-second delay detonators, the whole face was blasted in one go. Half-second delays allowed you to count the shots as they went off. If you heard a gap you knew that there had been a misfire (an explosive charge that has failed to go off) and had to check the charges very closely once you went back to the face. After the explosion fifteen minutes were given to allow the dust and fumes to be drawn out by an exhaust fan that was positioned at the return airway.

When the drifters returned they would advance two straight steel girders that hung from hooks from the previously set mine girders. On to these straight girders they would place girders known as the crown section. Each girder consisted of a crown and two legs. This secured the roof, allowing the drifters to start working. Three of them would then set up two drilling machines on top of the debris from the blasting which would be lying nearly to the roof and start to bore the top holes of the tunnel. Then another two would get the Emco Loaders ready. These were small compressed air driven mechanical loaders on rails which were driven into the debris with their buckets down. Once the debris was in the bucket it was lifted over their heads and loaded into the mine cars which were coupled to them at their rear.

In full flight these little Emcos buzzed in and out at a fair rate and once the mine cars were full they were taken away from the Emcos by a small rope haulage over a crossing on to the full track and then another empty car was pushed in to be coupled on to the Emco. This continued until all the debris had been cleaned up and the girder legs set on to the crowns and secured using wooden props. The drifters then set up four or five drilling machines and started to bore the face. This took about an hour and a half and the noise was terrible - if you were in there for any length of time it took ages for your hearing to get back to normal.

The full mine cars were hauled out to the pit bottom by a smelly little diesel loco. The driver stood in the middle of the loco and operated the controls. It was a pure pig to start as you had to turn a starting handle, cranking it round and round until the engine fired (but if it decided to kick back it just about broke your wrist).

The drifters carried their explosives down the pit in ammunition boxes, four boxes each, ten pounds per box. On one shift, as the drifters were walking in from the pit bottom, chatting amongst themselves, one of them failed to notice that the NCB workers had made a pit for a new loader. This pit was about five feet deep and was lying full of water and the drifter was so engrossed in the chit-chat that he walked right into it. One of his boxes burst open and there he was floundering about in the water with sticks of explosives floating around him. All his mates were falling about in stitches.

My method for blasting the tunnel was as follows. I would make up the primer detonators and the drifters would charge the shot holes. After this was completed myself and the supervisor would couple up the shots, each of us starting at opposite ends. They had to be connected in a certain way with each one linked to the one next to it, up and down the face in series until we met in the middle. In the middle of the pattern was a section called the burn cut. This consisted of nine holes being drilled, three on the top, three in the middle and three at the bottom, with only two of the top three and one in the centre and two in the bottom being charged using three and a half pounds of explosives in each hole with No.0 detonators. This section blew out first and as its name suggested it burnt the centre out; the rest of the explosive charges blew into the centre, in a circle, up to No.15 detonators in the corner which went off last. When the connections were completed they were coupled to the main shotfiring cable. A test was carried out for continuity to make sure everything was okay and we would then go out to the shotfiring station two hundred yards out the tunnel. I always made sure that the drifters were away from the face before the shots were coupled together. Then the supervisor and I went out to the station where, using a multi-shotfiring battery capable of setting off one hundred shots, I would set off the charges.

One of the other shotfirers, Ken, was on the shift that followed ours. He told me of a near thing that happened to him. After charging up the face and coupling on to the main cables, he and the supervisor and drifters walked out to the firing station. Ken coupled on the exploder, but before turning the key he decided to have a head count and found that one drifter was missing. The supervisor said he was away to do the toilet out in the mine but when Ken looked for the light of the man's lamp he could not see it. By this time the supervisor was getting impatient, telling Ken to get the shots fired. Ken was still not happy so he uncoupled the shots from the exploder, had another look to check the mine but still he couldn't see any light. So he started back into the face. The supervisor by now was going spare. "I'll claim a delay off you," he was saying but Ken kept on walking back in. He was right in at the crossing when he spotted a light at the far side of the mine cars and found the drifter putting timber over the compressed air pipes to protect them from the blast. When Ken spoke to him all the guy said was, "Are you ready to fire?" He had no idea that they had gone out and were ready to blast two hundred pounds of explosive charges with him still inside. They would only have found little pieces of him and as for the supervisor, he didn't know what to say or where to look. Obviously, it paid to be very diligent when using explosives.

During the time I was in the South Lateral Mine I was also shot-firing for the Cementation Company at the 333 fathom level. I discovered that only one of the small cages could be entered from the pit bottom there as the concrete of the shaft had been laid too far round. The Cementation decided that they were going to try and widen the shaft by tunnelling around the concrete with a six feet by six feet tunnel. I was sent to fire this tunnel and when I got there the supervisor, who I didn't know, had the face all drilled including the burn cut. When I started to stem up the holes he told me how much explosive he wanted in each one. I was no longer the green rookie shotfirer and told him I was quite capable of weighing the charges correctly and disagreed with the amount he wanted to put in. He told me he was the supervisor and he gave the orders. We had a bit of an argument so I sent for the deputy who surprised me by telling me to do what the supervisor wanted. I charged up the shots and again told him they were too heavily charged before firing the round.

After the dust had cleared, I went in and checked the face and then went out to the shaft to return to the 1,600 level. On the way I noticed the girders across the shaft had started to bend inward - the heavy blasting had disturbed the sides of the shaft and they had started to move in. I made a hasty retreat to the upper level and left them to it. I learned later that one of the other shotfirers had fired a series of holes along the floor of the pit bottom, leading to the shaft. This area was about thirty feet long, supported by twenty feet straight girder legs and thirty feet top girders. When this area was fired the feet of the straight girders started to slip into the excavation, so possibly this had an effect on the shaft as well. I bet the supervisor didn't last long after those little episodes.

I was never back at the 333 level so I don't know exactly what happened after that, only that the developing there stopped. I must have worked in the South Lateral for about a year and I reckoned it was in about a mile. They did develop a face in at the Lochgelly

Splint which could only be approached up a steep incline although the face itself was level. The experts came from either Edinburgh or London, carried out some test and then pronounced that the face line was unsuitable for machine mining so it was closed. All the girders which had been placed were left intact and a brick wall was built at the start of the mine to block it off. What a waste.

I was moved to the new face developments in the Cardenden section. The coal there was very faulted and water was always present in the section. At the main tunnel there was a fissure in the side of the tunnel where water used to pour out as if from a tap. We would fill our water bottles with it as it was crystal clear and tasted great. Newcomers to the section were warned not to drink this water straight after they came off the faces as it was ice cold. Most took our advice, but there was always the odd idiot who would have a big drink and then double up with stomach cramp within a minute or so. Eventually the Cardenden was closed altogether because the coal was so faulted.

I think it was about this time that the Auchengiech disaster occurred. I had left home for the afternoon shift when the news was announced on the television. Man riding bogies which were travelling down a dipping ran into a fire and forty-seven men perished. Auchengiech was at Chryston, not far from Cardowan. I used to get the Auchengiech pit bus to the Cardowan road end every morning so I knew a lot of the miners there. Among those who died was one of the lads I knew from Twechar and some of the other men working at Rothes lost relatives in this disaster. I had a friend who was in one of the mine rescue teams at the colliery. He told me his team brought the first body out, a horrific experience. The miners had all died instantly from inhaling whitedamp gas before they had reached the fire.

My mate and his team were wearing a breathing apparatus known as Prototype Mark 4. This only had a mouth piece and nose clips and the wearers in this case felt as if they were going to be sick; indeed, the minute they reached the fresh air base and handed over the stretcher, they had to pull off their apparatus so that they could throw up. Before they had gone down, the superintendent of the Mines Rescue Station at Coatbridge had warned them of the task ahead and promised them a brandy when they reached the surface. But when the management and senior officials saw the first body it was they who got the brandy. All the miners were identified by their lamp numbers and put in lead lined coffins right away - their relatives did not even see them. At the funerals the turnout was so great that loudspeakers were used to relay the service to the crowds outside.

NINE
ROTHES, 1960

I went back to the Lochgelly Splint to work with my favourite over-man once more. The section was going uphill and was a developing section for the whole district as new coal faces were opened up all along the right hand side. The two face conveyors emptied on to a special pan which was seven feet wide at the face end and narrowed down to two feet where it joined on to a column of jigging pans. This was how the coal was taken from the face to the loader.

As this face proceeded uphill it opened up facelines on the right hand side. The first section that I had worked in the Lochgelly was now shortened from the main gate up the left side only. It was now a power loading face with a more up to date version of the plough that was in Cardowan. It was pulled up and down the face by means of an endless steel chain instead of the haulage ropes and was nicknamed the 'Ambo Hobo', which derived from its German name.

This face had a lot of geological problems and the roof would often collapse. One day, during a particularly bad roof movement, it started to come down towards the pans and the face equipment. The miners were trying to secure it and were not having much success when my favourite overman decided to do his bit. He started to saw props and place them below the roof as it was coming down. The full width of the roof was coming in and as soon as he placed a prop it would take the weight and then break. The facemen decided it was time to get out, but not him. He just kept sawing and placing the props, but they kept breaking and the roof got lower and lower. The men were shouting at him to get out and the deputy ordered him off the face at once. There was a terrible roaring noise as all the face props started smashing and then the roof fell down altogether. The idiot managed to get out, but only just by the skin of his teeth.

On the Lochgelly No.1 I worked with two other shotfirers and a deputy. It was here that I had an unofficial shotfiring accident. I was firing the face at the main gate and there was a fault up about ten yards on the left side. I charged up five holes altogether - which was a wee bit naughty of me as I was only supposed to fire one at a time - and being a bit of a smartie pants I tried to fire all five together. Two went off leaving three unfired so I coupled them up and tried again. Still only two went off and I was left with one right in the middle. I sent my sentries away once more and when they shouted that they were ready I went out and fired the last shot. After everything was clear, I returned up the face to fire more places.

A short while later the deputy came up and told me one of the men, Charlie, had come to him with a lump of coal stuck in his buttock. Charlie was saying that the coal that had hit him had been dislodged from one of the pans, and that it was nothing to do with the shotfiring, but the deputy said he knew what a shotfiring wound looked like and he was sure this was one. I was told that Charlie had gone away up the pit to see the nurse and was going to report it. I asked the deputy what he was going to do and he said he would just wait.

When I got to the surface the undermanager and my favourite overman were waiting on me. They accused me of having a shotfiring accident and not reporting it. I said as far as I was concerned I didn't have an accident and would wait and see what the stripper had to say about it. They replied that Charlie was saying he was struck by coal off the pans, but that they knew better so I had better admit what I had done. I told them in no uncertain manner that I was not going to admit to something I hadn't done and they were not pleased.

I spoke to Charlie a couple of days later and he told me what had actually happened. "It was all my own fault," he said, "when you told me to go back up the face, I curled up just at the start and put my lamp out. I shouted I was ready and when you fired, a piece of coal hit me. No way was I going to let anyone know what an idiot I had been or get you into trouble over my own stupidity." Charlie should have made sure he was much further out of the way but he admitted himself that it was his own fault, so again I was lucky to have a stripper like that working beside me.

We worked one week on the backshift and one on the dayshift and we fired the brushings and the hitches as well as a couple of waste drivages. On the backshift I worked with an older shotfirer who I'll call Robbie. He always carried sweets and said they were the "bestest". They were usually treacle or licorice centres. One day as I was preparing to fire the main gate, Robbie came up and was very distressed. When I asked what was wrong, he told me that as he was going into one of the waste drivages he smelled cigarette smoke. When he got right in he discovered the developers smoking and when he challenged them about it they told him to get lost. As he was on his own there was nothing he could do about it. I said that we should go and see about it and we went back to this road. The men were there and when I spoke to them, they called Robbie a liar. The leading man stuck his face right into mine and said, "What are you going to do about it?" so I hit him straight in the mouth, bursting his lip and loosening a couple of teeth. I didn't stop at one punch, but laid him out on the floor of the tunnel. I then turned to his mates and asked who was next. Robbie had to come between me and them or I might have committed murder. "Where I come from you would be dead meat," I told them, "You've obviously never worked in a gassy pit or you wouldn't be smoking underground." I then went back to fire the main gate but Robbie was worried in case the guy reported me. "Let him," I said, "After all he did attack me, didn't he?" Whereupon Robbie started to laugh.

By March I was firing the old main gate. The tunnel was being enlarged to make it a locomotive road so that a new loader could be installed. I was using instantaneous detonators so I could only fire six at a time and once I had fired the side shots all my detonators were used up. Another shotfirer was sent to give me a hand to finish the job. I stood on the debris from the blasting of the sides and had started to stem up the top holes when the roof collapsed. I was hit across the face and as I turned to get away, I saw the other shotfirer standing rooted to the spot. I turned and pushed him out of the way of the roof fall. Then the whole lot decided to fall on top of me. My helmet was knocked off my head and I was plunged into total darkness as rocks started to fall on me. I felt them strike me on my back and then I went down underneath them. My legs were being forced down between two rocks, tearing them as they were pushed in. All the back brushers had ran for their lives as the tunnel started to collapse and when the roof stopped caving in, silence came and the brushers returned to find out what had happened to me. They found me lying face down covered in debris, but I was still alive. I reckon that once again my guardian angel had looked after me.

The brushers started to dig me out but there was a very large rock lying on top of my legs which they couldn't lift off. They got wooden straps and using them as levers they eased up the rock. I had to turn over on to my back and easing my torn leg out from between the two rocks, the men pulled me clear. They sat me down on an ammunition box and the deputy came to take a look at my leg. The flesh and skin were right down over my boot and my shin bone was shining in the light, as clean as a whistle. The sight of all this blood and flesh was too much for the deputy and he went away to be sick.

The face overman, George Parker, arrived on the scene to see what had happened to me. This man saved my leg. He took some large dressings from my first aid box (we all carried a metal first aid box on our belts as it was part of our job to render assistance to anyone who required it) and slowly he lifted the flesh and skin back into place, padded it up with the dressings, and put me on a stretcher to be carried to the pit bottom and then to the surface. If he hadn't have done these things I doubt if I would have been able to continue my life as a miner. When I arrived at the pit bottom I asked George to turn the stretcher around and he asked me why. "If I'm put into the cage this way, I'll come out at the surface feet first. I come from Cardowan where only dead men come out feet first, and I'm not dead yet so just turn me around." George laughed at me for being superstitious and turned my stretcher around.

When I arrived at the medical room, the colliery sister cut off the bandages, took one look and ordered the men to get me into the waiting ambulance. She told the orderly that she was going to the hospital with me. I felt every bump in the road but eventually we reached the hospital. My leg was X-rayed and a little while later a doctor came in to show me the plates. There was nothing broken so he would stitch me up and send me home. I was then given a jag and taken into the theatre. The first thing I heard was the theatre sister getting at somebody because I was still in my dirty pit clothes. She wasn't long in cutting them off. The anaesthetist came up and gave me a second jag. "Sleepy?" she asked, but I said no so she gave me another jag, this time into my bent wrist. "Sleepy?" she asked again as she took the rubber tube off my arm. I was going to speak, but the next thing I knew was coming round, lying on a blanket, with a nurse asking me for my dummy. There was a rubber thing in my mouth, it was the airway that they had put in to stop my tongue from slipping down my throat during the operation.

Once I was fully conscious the nurse came back with a basin of water and gave me an all over wash and some time later the doctor came in to see me. He said I had been given twenty-one stitches in my leg, three in my nose and a couple in my forehead. Also, the wound was a little bit worse than he first thought, so he was going to keep me in for a couple of days.

When I awoke I found my leg had been put on an elevation and the dressing was needing to be changed. That was when I met Staff Nurse Wilson. She came in, eyes smiling behind a surgical mask, saying "Good morning". She dressed my wound and we had a bit of a chat. She told me she came from Lenzie, her first name was Elsa and she did some of her training in Glasgow. She asked about my family and when I told her my daughter Janice was only a month old she was very interested. I ended up staying in hospital for two weeks and over that time we had quite a few chats. When I left I made a date with Elsa to come to our home so that she could bath Janice. We have been good friends ever since that time.

Six weeks later I was back at work. On my first shift I had to go under the brushing that had fallen on me which gave me a funny sensation. It was on this face that I realised that what the government inspector had told me a couple of years earlier about looking up the face before firing was very good advice. I had charged up a couple of holes in this stripper's place; they were his first shots of the shift and had thirteen ounces of explosive in each. He went away up the face and I went down. This face was only three feet high and had a four and a half foot undercut. The shots would bring down about three tons of coal, right across to the pans. After I was ready, I decided to have a last look up the face and I saw a miner crawling down the face. I went to meet him and we met right at the shot holes. It was the union man and when I asked where he was going, he said "To the main gate, I've a meeting this morning with Matt Peden to discuss a complaint." I asked him to look up and when he did his face turned white. I asked if he had seen the sentry. "Saw him - I spoke to him as I went past." So we both approached the sentry and what the union man called him can't be printed. The union man thanked me for my diligence and from that day on I always looked up before firing any shots.

The faces being developed on the right hand side of the Lochgelly were opened up and a new machine called an Anderson Boyes Shearer was installed. This was even better than the Samson Stripper and had a drum with picks which was rotated, cutting off the coal while the machine hauled itself up and down the run. Unfortunately, the faults in these faces made use of this shearer impractical. The plough was also taken out and a shearer put in its place, to see if the drum with its twenty inch cut would help to support the roof. Allowing the props to be moved in, Dowty hydraulic props were being used along with three feet hinged bars. The shearer could only cut one way then plough back so the conveyor was pushed over during the ploughing. This meant that the supports had to wait until the ploughing was in progress before they could be advanced. Again this proved to be a disadvantage as the faulted roof caved in more often making life more difficult for the miners. As No.1 kept going uphill, I wondered why the powers that be didn't consider driving the old main gate straight in, thus developing another uphill face and so on, so that the faults would run off as the faces advanced.

However, No.1 faceline continued through faulted ground. The dayshift had not been able to strip all the coal, so it had been left to the backshift to finish off. This had a knock-on effect. When we came out the next day, we had to shift the pans left from the backshift. I was sent to supervise a group of strippers. After sitting a while at the start of the shift in the tail gate, they went on to the face. Then after shifting a couple of pans, they decided to have a game of cards. When I told them that this was not on, I got a mouthful of abuse so I went to get their leading man to talk to them (if I told my favourite overman he would have blown a gasket). I found the leading man, told him the state of play and guess what he did? He told the deputy, who went flying up the face in a rage. As we approached the fault we could see them playing cards. The deputy went in as if he was jet propelled. "Right," he told them, "Your time is stopped." There was a bit of an argument and the strippers went off the face. They were only gone about a minute before they came back saying, "where's the cards then, we don't have any." They had obviously disposed of them so that there was no evidence against them but the deputy sent them up the pit anyway.

We went about our business for the rest of the shift and when we reached the surface at the end of it we were told to report to the general manager's office. He was a new man, a Mr Duncan. When we got there the strippers were in along with their union man. I was asked to tell my version of events, but the men said I was lying and so was the deputy. The general manager lost his temper at this - "My officials are not liars, so I am closing the section right now. The backshift will start to remove the plant [coal face machinery] immediately." The irony of this was that the left side had increased to a height of four foot six inches of coal so there was plenty of it still to be mined. I had a gut feeling that this kind of trouble would lead to the demise of the Rothes.

Along with another shotfirer I was sent to the Five Foot Lateral which was now a shearer face and I teamed up with my old mate Ken from the South Lateral mine. One day as Ken was firing the top coal around a fault, he stemmed up five holes, stopping the pans before going up to the firing station. As he was coupling on to the exploder the pans started up. The top coal fell off the roof on to the pans and when he tried to stop the conveyor it kept on going. He looked over the face and as he could still see the detonator wires, he thought the explosives were still in the face. However, when he eventually got the conveyor stopped and checked over the face again he found that the primers with the detonators in them had fallen into the pans and had gone down the loader and into the mine cars. As a result, he had to number the mine cars and escort them to the surface where they were emptied by hand. I got to the surface at nine o'clock and Ken was still emptying the mine cars - nobody had been sent to help him. He had found three out of the five primers when it was time to go home and when he went to put his lamp away there was a letter giving him one month's notice.

Next day Ken went to see Mr Barrie, explaining that he was the shotfirer who had lost the primers. "Have you been to the union yet?" Mr Barrie asked him.

"No," Ken replied, "I'm waiting to see you first."

"Well come back on Wednesday."

So Ken went back on Wednesday, was asked the same questions and told to come back on Friday. This went on until the month's notice was about up. On the last day he went in to see Mr Barrie, he got the same questions, and then finally was asked what had happened.

"Why didn't you stop the pans right away?" Mr Barrie asked.

"Somebody just kept them going and they wouldn't stop."

Mr Barrie asked who would be responsible for this. Ken had a good idea but wouldn't say; he had his suspicions about an overman but had no proof. Finally, Mr Barrie told him to get back to work - he was giving him a last shot at the coconuts and the matter was closed.

Ten

Rothes, 1961 - 1962

It was decided by the top management to start driving two large mines away from the 1,600 feet level towards the 333 fathom level or beyond until they reached the Hirst seam. Smaller roadways had already been driven to the dip and these were now enlarged to take twenty feet by twelve feet arch girders to support the roof. After this was completed, work on driving the main mines began.

As in the South Lateral mine, the face was bored with around ninety holes and about two hundred pounds of explosives were used. These mines were going to the dip at a gradient of one in five, making the loading of the debris from the blasting difficult. This was overcome by introducing the use of caterpillar tracked Emco shovels with a hopper attached to them at the back. The shovel would drive into the debris and load the hopper. Then it would reverse uphill to the steel conveyor, empty the hopper on to it and then drive back down again, a process which was repeated until all the debris from the blasting was removed. When the face was ready to fire again the Emco was turned around so that its controls were protected from the blast.

Working with us were drifters who had been with the Cementation Company, but were now transferred to the NCB. Unfortunately, they still drilled the burn cut pattern which was not very suitable for firing mines that were dipping. One day the face was all charged up, the Emco had been turned away from the direction of the blast, and the drifters and the shotfirer had retired to the firing station. After firing the shots they returned to the face to discover that the burn cut had come out in one solid mass which had struck the Emco in the middle, buckling the steel shovel. The undermanager was not pleased about this when he was told and it was decided that a tunnelling expert would be brought in to produce a drilling pattern to suit the dips.

Several patterns were tried before we eventually came up with a drag cut in the centre instead of the burn cut. This pattern consisted of a line of short holes bored along the bottom at an angle, then a row of longer holes drilled above them at a lesser angle, and another row above these again, and so on, until a pull of seven feet would come out from the centre. This allowed two girders to be set three feet apart.

The mines were advanced in this way until there was a need for another conveyor to be installed and we progressed quite well until we reached the notorious millstone grit, an area of water-bearing sandstone which had been encountered during the sinking of the shafts. It also contained some very faulted ground. During a shift I was on, the drifters were boring the top holes off the top of the newly fired face. They were using a compressed air borer with an airleg to assist in holding the drilling machine up. This was a big change from type of borer I first used and it even passed water through the drilling rod which washed the drillings out as well as keeping the dust down. One of the drillers named Eck was at the controls and as he was drilling and approaching seven feet in, water started to come out of the hole. He thought that the drill's water pressure had been increased so he shouted to his mate Mitch to turn it off, but water was still coming out of the bore hole. Eck shouted at Mitch once more, when suddenly, boring machine, seven foot drill and Eck were lifted away from the hole, followed by a flood of water. The dipping tunnel started to fill up with water and it kept rising until the whole face was submerged.

The water rose steadily for the rest of the shift and travelled up as far as the steel pans. We moved the Emco up as far as it could go and when we left at the end of our shift the water level was not moving up so fast. During the following shift it stopped but then there was the problem of pumping out the tunnel. An Evans pump arrived a couple of shifts later. This was capable of pumping out the water from the dipping to the main lateral mine into the gauton (a watercourse cut in the pavement of a mine or working) that ran into the pit bottom pump house. It was about nine feet long, three feet broad and seven feet high and contained a large water vessel similar in shape to the vessel in the middle of a steam locomotive, although a bit bigger. It didn't take long for it to pump out the mine, and then we went back in to clean up the face and set the girders.

The face was drilled once more and charged up, with yours truly to be the first to fire with this monster of a pump right in front. I inquired if there had been any arrangements made to either move the pump or to protect it from the blasting, but I was told to cover it over with wooden straps and props and get on with it. As I coupled up the wires of the face charges, I sent the men up to collect timber and they covered up the pump until it couldn't be seen for wood. As I retired to the firing station, I was still apprehensive about it but I coupled up the battery and turned the key. As the round went off, mingled with the noise of the explosion I heard an unusual sound like the clanking of metal. After the dust had settled I went down toward the face and just below the firing station I came across the large water vessel. It had been blown off and had travelled over a hundred yards. The timber that had been covering it was scattered about like pieces of match wood. "Well," I thought, "that's me in trouble again".

We now had an English undermanager and he was not enamoured with us unco-operative Scots. When I arrived at the surface I was sent for. "Please explain how you managed to destroy a piece of expensive equipment?" I was asked. I nearly answered "quite easily" but thought better of it. Instead, I said, "Well sir, we covered it with wood, but this turned out to be inadequate."

"What do you mean covered it in wood? Why didn't you use the steel wire net I sent down to the dips?"

"I didn't get a net or even knew there was one available." I answered, but he didn't believe me and went away to see the surface foreman only to discover the net was still lying on the surface waiting on a destination to be marked on it. "You're off the hook," the undermanager told me, "but I'll be watching you."

When we started driving through the millstone grit, we encountered more problems. The seven foot holes wouldn't blast the face, they would only blow out the shot hole, making a larger hole. This meant that we had to drill the face again with short four feet holes, then fire it until we could get a girder up and then we had to repeat this operation until we could put the second girder up. We contin-

ued drilling four feet holes and getting at least four feet of tunnelling done each shift. This did not please the Pharaoh (as we
called the undermanager) so he told us to revert to the old method.
He told us that since we seemed incapable of doing it he would per-
sonally come underground to show us how to charge up this type of
face. He did this on a couple of shifts and the results were worse
than our best. He was not pleased, so started to change primers
around during the charging up, leaving the shotfirers with a tangle
of detonator wires (each detonator had about nine feet of wire
attached to it) to deal with.

One day it was my turn to be visited by this so-called expert and
right away it was "give me this - no - change that - I want this".
Nevertheless, the face would not pull seven foot when fired. He
then went away up the pit, leaving me to try and salvage the mess.
This went on for a couple of shifts until I lost my temper - I threw
the detonator bag containing one hundred detonators minus the
ones he had messed up at him, telling him to make up his own
primers. He took one look at me then went away. I finished charging the face, fired it, and by then it was time to go up the pit. Next
morning my nightshift neighbour told me we needed a circuit tester
as the one we were using had packed in. I went to the magazine to
get one, only to be told there were no repaired ones available. I
would need a line to get a new one so I went to the undermanager
for this. "You won't need one," he told me and when I inquired why,
I was told to give my detonator bag to a deputy who he had been
instructed to take my place. I told him that no way was I drawing
a detonator bag to give to anyone else. "Fine," he said, "don't both-
er," and with that he started to walk away.

"So where do I go?" I asked.

"You can do as you damn well please because you are not working
in my area."

I just stood there feeling like a right wally until Mr Barrie came
along. "What have you been up to this time?" he asked me. I told
him the full story. "You're a bit of a hothead aren't you!" he said and
I had to agree with him - what else could I do?

"Come with me," he said and we both went to the shaft and went
underground. The undermanager was down the dips when we

arrived so Mr Barrie sent for him. When he appeared Mr Barrie told him "If anyone is going to be disciplined in my pit then I will do it. In the meantime Ian goes back to his work so tell the deputy to give him back his detonator bag so that he can get on with the job I employ him to do."

The undermanager was about to argue, but changed his mind. So I stayed until we reached the Hirst seam, which was around the beginning of 1962.

During the time I was in the dips I attended Kirkcaldy Technical college to obtain the new Deputies Certificate. I passed the course and got my certificate in March 1962. The men of the pit were also quite excited when the Hirst was reached as this was the area of development which would help to save our pit. But this was not to be. Mr Stewart, the area production manager, came for an inspection and told us that while this was the right area for development, it would cost five million pounds to create productive coal faces and he didn't think that the NCB in London would sanction it. Also, by this time the world market for coal was falling and British Railways were changing from steam to cheaper diesel-powered engines. In the meantime the men of Rothes were left with two mines and no further development until London made a decision.

While waiting on developments on the dips the Five Foot Lateral face struck the white stone as it was called. It was a giant fault and the coal started to disappear in the bottom corner of the face, to be replaced by solid rock. Within a couple of shifts the whole face had turned into a rock face and the usual method of drilling up into the roof and then drilling down into the floor was used to try and locate the coal. When this failed Mr Barrie asked if he could drive a mine from the main gate at the gradient calculated from the surface boreholes but this was not allowed by the bosses in Edinburgh and London.

I was sent by the undermanager to salvage the bottom end of the Five Foot Lateral section. This was his revenge for Mr Barrie's interference when he had tried to get rid of me. The first job was to remove a pump from a small dipping off from the bottom tail gate. The dipping had a steady flow of water dropping down from the roof. I was to supervise the withdrawal of this pump and found that there was only one man to help me who during the war had been a prisoner in a Japanese camp. He was quite old and not very strong and I was quite shocked that he had been given this job - what a way to treat someone like that. I asked him why he was even down a pit and he told me it was his pride: "They didn't break me in Burma, so no way was I going to let them beat me at home. I've been on light work for years, looking after pumps and things, but the only mistake I made was to transfer from Balgonie to this shit-house of a pit." At Balgonie it seemed that everybody helped everybody else, something that reminded me of Cardowan and I had to agree with him that working at Rothes was a very different experience. In the end we eventually got the pump out and up to the surface.

Other areas of the Five Foot were opened up, but to no avail as they kept running into faulted ground. Soon all the options ran out and in April we were told that the Rothes was to close. On hearing the news, some miners staged a sit-in which I think was the first in Scotland, if not the whole of Britain. I got my redundancy notice which would come into effect in April 1964. Some miners were transferred to the Wellsley, Michael and Frances Collieries, but all that was on offer to us NUM shotfirers was oncost work or counting steel props and making sure none were left in the waste. As I was a face worker before I became a shotfirer I felt this was a bit unfair, so I opted to transfer to an English pit along with a couple of mates of mine, George Howard, and Jim Reid who actually joined the pit with me in 1958 and we've been mates ever since. In the early days at the Rothes he had digs around the corner from me and I used to walk round each morning to wake him up. If I hadn't done that he would never have made the dayshift!

We applied for a transfer to Thurcroft Colliery in Rotherham. We travelled down to Jim's mother-in-law's house there and then went to see the assistant manager of the colliery. When we went in to see him he immediately recognised Jim who had worked in the pit before going to Rothes. Foreign labour was not allowed in this particular pit and at that time there were a lot of Poles working in British pits, so when I was introduced to him he asked if I was one. I just about choked. "No," I said, "I'm Scottish through and through."

"Sorry," he said, "I've not heard the name Terris before but we had a man in here called Smith and he turned out to be a Pole. Brought whole pit out on strike."

Eleven

Thurcroft, 1962

One morning in April Jim, George, and I arrived at the pithead of Thurcroft for a seven o'clock start. We carried a five pint water container called a 'duddly' and descended the shaft. At the pit bottom we took off our jackets and hung them on nails set in wood at the side of the shaft. We walked away from the bottom around a corner and it was like entering a blast furnace - the heat was terrific. Boarding a set of bogies, we descended a steep dipping and on dismounting we followed the rest of the miners to the meeting station (a place where men meet before they disperse to their work following a safety examination by their deputy).

We were spare 'market men' to be used in any type of face work. As we sat there the overman came over and spoke to us. He told me in his Yorkshire accent that I was to go to 89's. I asked where that was as this was my first shift in the pit. He turned to one of the miners who was passing and said, "Take Jock to 89's."

"But I'm going to 82's," was the reply.

"Take Jock to 89's, then go to 82's."

This was my first insight into the power the officials in this pit had over the men. The miner just shrugged and said, "Come on." We went away to another tunnel and a short time later a train of bogies pulled by a haulage rope, known as a 'paddy train', came into the end where we were standing. It consisted of several bogies coupled together and each one had about six groups of four seats, two facing two. We climbed aboard and off it went. After a long distance we got off and transferred to another paddy (they both worked on the same rope and met in the middle) and this went further in the same distance again. When we disembarked the miner told me to strip off and I asked if we were going to get a medical. He looked at me rather puzzled and said the men there always stripped to their shorts because of the heat - and he wasn't kidding, I was sweating just standing still. So there I was, stripped down to my under pants, a helmet on my head and a pair of Wellington boots on my feet (what a sight!). I rolled up my clothes and put them behind a girder like the rest of them. We started to walk along another tunnel up to our ankles in limestone dust (an inert dust which was laid on roads to cover coal dust and reduce its flammability in the event of an explosion). After a while we reached a junction in the tunnels. He told me to go up a rise through the screen and I would be there. Then he went off back to the 82's where he was the hole borer.

I went up the rise and through the screen and came to the top stable. I went on to the face where there were three strippers and they asked if I had come to work with them. I said I had and one of them said, "We're waiting on the fitter to sort this bloody machine." It was an undercutting coal cutter and when I asked what was wrong he said that it kept on jamming and that the chain probably needed tightening. I asked for a shovel - "A what?" - so I pointed at one - "Oh! you mean a spade!" I started to shovel the gum away from the cutting picks and told them to try the machine again. It started to cut and I kept shovelling away the gum cuttings so it wouldn't jam up. When I looked up they were standing there watching me. I told them that that was all they had to do to keep the cutter going, but the leading man, Dennis, just said "Only a daft bloody Scot would shovel behind picks." Then he shouted for the fitter who eventually came and tightened up the chain. When I asked them when they stopped for their piece again they didn't seem to understand. Pointing at my mouth I said "Eat" and they said, "Oh! Snap." I thought they wanted to play cards. "Whenever you're hungry Jock, just go and eat," they said, but I decided that it would be safer just to eat whenever they did.

After the face was cut Dennis told me and another man, Bernie, to put up a couple of 'dowties' (hydraulic props consisting of two telescoping steel cylinders extended by hydraulic pressure which was provided by a hand-operated pump built into the prop) and bars. While we were doing this, Dennis and the other men would go and have their snap and then would come back to bore the face, at which point we could go and eat. When our turn came, I sat down beside Bernie as he opened his box and took out a roll. It looked as if it had come straight out of a frying pan and was all melted, a piece 'in dripping'. My own piece was pan bread with butter and jam and it was just a soggy mess, but I was hungry so it disappeared *tout suite*.

We hadn't been sitting for long when the screen flew back and these two apparitions in brown shirts and breeches, carrying hand lamps, came upon us. "What thou doing?" one of them demanded in a thick Yorkshire accent. "We're snapping, Mr Stevenson," said little Bernie. I thought he was going to kiss their boots he was so low. "Eleven o'clock in day and your snapping?" the man roared. Here we go again, I thought, another loony.

He was shining his lamp in our eyes, something which can be very off-putting so I told him so. "You can't say that to the assistant manager," Bernie spluttered, but I said, "I'll make him swallow the bleeding thing if he doesn't stop shining it at me."

"Who are you then and where do you come from?" Mr Stevenson demanded and when I told him Rothes, he replied, "That were pit Queen went down, weren't it?"

"Yes," I said.

"It didn't last long did it. Well, don't be long," and with that he went on to the face. The colliery overman with him gave me a dirty look as they left. Turning to Bernie, I saw half a roll disappearing into his mouth in a one gulp. Then he went straight back on to the face. I went on just after him. The assistant manager was watching us like a hawk. We fired the face and cleaned most of it up before it was time to walk back to where my clothes were. I put them on and went away to the pit bottom to get my jacket and go to the surface. The end of my first shift of serfdom at Thurcroft.

The next morning we reported to the overman. Jim and I were sent to 82's to do the brushing, or 'ripping' as they called it. We travelled in on the paddy, got stripped off and put our clothes behind the girders and set off for the face. After about half an hour's walk we arrived at the tail gate. A miner came out towards us - he looked like a POW from the war. His ribs were sticking out and he was wheezing like an old cart horse. "Have you come to rip with us?" he rasped and we said we had. He went back to the face, got a compressed air rotary borer and set it up. We started to bore the face and within a minute you couldn't see for the dust - no wonder the man's lungs were knackered. We bored six holes and went on to the face to prepare the edges of the road, setting props along the lip of the brushing, and when we were ready the shotfirer came and fired the holes.

After the shots had been fired we went into the face. The biggest piece of redd at the lip measured about six inches. "This strata is very poor and always comes down like this," the man told us. "There are steel mesh bags, about half the size of a coal bag - you fill them with the debris from the lip and build them up like a wall, filling any gaps with any debris that's left." So Jim and I set to work, filling some of the bags and setting the back end. I started to shovel the debris back to Jim and after every shovelful, poor Jim disappeared in a cloud of dust, coughing and spluttering.

After a while, working away, we saw this light coming up the coal face. It was a man approaching, but there was something out of the ordinary about him, and then Jim exclaimed, "Look, he's naked!" It was a miner, helmet on his head, belt around his waist to hold his lamp, a pair of boots on his feet and nothing, absolutely nothing, else on. I felt like the guy in the song 'Don't look Ethel'. He was shifting steel props to allow the coal cutter to undercut the face (it was a hand-stripped face). The heat was terrific right enough, so you could understand the reason behind this unusual sight.

We eventually got the brushing packs in (which served as pillars to support the roof) and the girder set and timbered up. Then it was time to trudge our way back to the paddy. We got our clothes and climbed aboard the next paddy to the pit bottom. Then we had a nice hot shower on the surface. The end of day two.

Day three started once more at the deputies meeting station where we were teamed up with two local men to go to 89's to shovel up the waste and build the packs on the face. The face here was a power loading face. It was firstly cut in the middle by a normal coal cutter, then the Huwood Slicer, as it was called, went up and down on an endless chain. This was similar to the plough, only it was mechanised and moved like a vibrating slicer taking a six inch slice at a time. We set to work and when we stopped for our piece, I felt water running down on to my shoulder. I looked up at the roof but couldn't see any signs of a leak. I told the other chap and he started to laugh. "It's coming out of your helmet." The sweat had soaked into the padding of my helmet and when it was saturated it came pouring out over my face.

The fourth day turned out to be my last shift in Thurcroft. I was feeling homesick and a sweat rash was starting to appear under my arm. I was sent into the 89's to do the same task that I had done the day before and I asked if I was to carry tools in with me. The overman said that the main gate brushers were there already (they started an hour before the rest of the facemen) and that they would give me tools when I got there. If there was any problem, I was just to tell them he said so. I travelled into the face where I met up with two sour faced individuals. "You come to work wae us?" one asked in his thick Yorkshire accent, and when I said I had he demanded to know where my tools were. I said they were to give me some and their reply took me aback - "Do you think that all we have to do is give tools to Bloody Jocks?"

"Please yourself," I said.

Finally, they told me to go out to the road where I would find a spade on a bar, so I got this - it had seen better days - and went on to the face. I asked for a hammer and was told, "We need it." I then asked for a pick and again the reply was, "We need it." So I said, "See this spade, you can shove it up your arse" and walked away.

The other facemen were sitting up the run listening and having a laugh at my expense. They came down and said, "Don't worry Jock, we don't even talk to them. What do you need?" and when I told them, they went and drew the dowties and bars for me.

I started to build the pack but there were not enough large stones to build the walls with. "Not to worry Jock, cutters on road up. We'll get you some." Right enough, once the coal cutter had passed they stopped the conveyor and pulled large stones off for me. All I could here was "Right, Jock" and another large stone was deposited alongside me. Eventually I started to build the pack and after I had the base built I started to shovel in any old material that was lying about, coal, stone and any other general rubbish. When Dennis came to see how I was doing he turned white, "Can't put coal in pack!" I asked why not and he told me that if the gaffer came down the run he would push his stick into the pack, and if he saw any coal in it he would condemn it. Then I would be reported and the manager would fine me. I asked if this happened a lot and he said it did. The upshot was that if I committed a couple of minor misdemeanours I would lose a shift's wages. I didn't like what I heard. Dennis gave me a hand to gather up stones to replace the coal I had lifted and rebuild the pack. As I was only wearing shorts my legs were all cut to ribbons and by the time we were done I was knackered.

At the end of the shift we walked out to the paddy where the lads were all laughing and joking, but I was wondering what I was doing there. I was a couple of hundred miles from home, likely to be on the waiting list for a house for at least a year and I couldn't face being in digs for all that time. I got on the paddy and on the road out I couldn't keep my eyes open, my head kept falling on to my knees. Eventually my helmet fell off my head on to the track. The shunter told me he'd get it for me on the next run; I thanked him and continued out to the pit bottom.

When I got to the surface and went for my shower I found my skin had all broken out in a rash, so I went to see the nurse. She offered me some cream for it and a supply of salt tablets. I told her that instead of the tablets she should just give me a ticket back to Scotland. By the time I had got back to my digs I had made up my mind. George, Jim and his mother-in-law helped me get enough money together for a ticket to Scotland and by midnight I was on the train with a parcel of sandwiches and a flask of tea, setting off for Edinburgh, then Kirkcaldy and home. At eight o'clock the next morning I got back and the first place I went to was the doctor who gave me a line to get out of the pits.

Twelve

Seafield, 1964 - 1965

February 1964 saw the birth of Mhairi, my second daughter. After getting out of the pits in '62 I got a job as a conductor with the W. Alexander bus company and was earning a living wage as long as I worked overtime. Mhairi was about two weeks old when I decided my wage packet couldn't support us. I had worked nearly a fortnight's hours for what would have been a week's wages in the mines. I made up my mind to see if I could get back into the pits and went to the NCB headquarters in Dysart to talk to Mr Gordon, the labour relations officer. He listened to my story and then got me an appointment with Mr Ludkin, the agent manager at Seafield. When I saw Ludkin he had already had a word with Mr Barrie who had given a good report about me, so all he wanted to know was when I could start. I told him a week on Monday and then the training officer took me along to get my check number, my lamp number, and my lockers.

The training officer showed me around the Seafield pithead. There were two shafts. One had a cage capable of carrying a hundred miners, fifty on each deck, as well as mine cars full of material. The other shaft had two skips capable of carrying fifteen tons each. The shafts had two levels, one at 170 fathoms and the other at 300 fathoms. As in the Rothes, everything was under cover from the moment you stepped in the main doors at the canteen. I was told that I would have to work five days along with another deputy to get my delayed action detonator certificate which would enable me to carry out the duties of a grade two deputy at Seafield.

On my first day I started at six in the morning, reporting to Bill Kennedy, the colliery overman, who teamed me up with another deputy called Willie McCormack. We went down the pit to the 300 fathom level and on arriving at the pit bottom we went into the man riding station. I saw six small mine cars attached to an electric locomotive and in the cars drifters were waiting on us. "Right," said Willie, "in we get." I looked into the mine car to see over six inches of water slopping about the floor with wooden straps floating around in it and I couldn't help noticing that the drifters were all wearing oilskins that had a cape attachment which made them look like batmen. "Sit on one of these straps if you can find a dry one," advised Willie, "As you can see we are all wearing oilskins as it's very wet inby. We'll get you a spare set when we get into the mine face." Well, there I was - the odd man out once more, sitting on a soaking wet strap with only a boiler suit on and six inches of water splashing over my boots.

With a jolt the train of cars took us away from the bright lights of the pit bottom into the pitch black of a large tunnel. About a quarter of a mile in we passed a loader that was lit up by fluorescent lamps - this was the Five Foot seam which was being developed to open up a coal face. We carried on past this and into what can only be described as a rainstorm, there was water pouring in everywhere. The drifters and Willie pulled up the flaps on their oilskin jackets to avoid getting wet but yours truly had nothing for protection so got ever so slightly wet (i.e. soaked). However, we passed through this and into the mine.

Seafield was driving through the infamous millstone grit as encountered in the Rothes. This time, however, the drifters had drilled a ninety yard pilot hole so that chemicals could be put in under pressure to seal the fissures and keep the water back, thus allowing the mine to be driven through the millstone in the normal manner. After the ninety yards had been advanced another pilot hole was bored and sealed and the mine blasted through once more, a procedure that was continued until the mine was through the wet area. The Five Foot and the Seven Foot seams were being developed out nearer the pit bottom. All transport was by electric locomotives, Metro Vicks and Greenbats. There were two types of mine cars, full sized ones like at Rothes and half size for transporting stone out of the mines (these carried three tons of stone).

Mine driving had changed since my days at the Rothes and the drilling pattern used was the drag cut. As in the Rothes dippings, a series of holes was bored along the bottom, then another row above at a different angle, then the same again until there were four rows. The bottom row consisted of No.0 detonators, the next row would be No.1 detonators and so on until the drag cut was charged up; the rest of the holes were then charged up in circles around the cut. When the face was fired the drifters bored the top holes as before, but instead of two small Emcos there was only one large Emco with a conveyor attached to the rear which loaded into the half cars, filling them evenly.

After I finished my five days and got the grade two certificate, I was put into the pit bottom to help with the transport on the dayshift and then was in charge of the pit bottom on the backshift. I would walk through the mines to check the gautons for any breaks in them or debris which might cause water to flood on to the rail tracks and go to the loco sheds to make sure all the loco batteries were charging. Then it was around to the main pump house to check that all was well. One time I found two young trainees fighting in the gauton and before I clipped them round their ears and sent them on their way (they were usually good lads so I didn't report them), I couldn't help smiling as I watched them slugging it out, up to their thighs in water.

Before I had arrived at Seafield they had opened a face in the Five Foot seam at the 170 level, but it was unsuitable for machine mining. It was then decided to develop a face at the 300 level. As I was the spare deputy, going wherever there was a deputy off, I had a spell in the Five Foot, blasting through a coal tunnel. It was a road with twelve feet by eight feet arch girders. There I used another type of detonator called the Carrick which had a millisecond delay suitable for blasting in coal. I worked in there for a couple of weeks and then the regular deputy returned so it was back to the bottom. A week after being moved on I was shocked to hear that one of the men I had been deputy to had been killed by a roof fall.

In 1965 I was sent to the 170 level to supervise the transporting of a new type of hydraulic roof support called the Gullick chock. I had two miners from Bowhill, one of whom was known as 'Bean' Bernard. I still know him today. He had a saying that he would come out with whenever I tried to push them to work harder - "You can take a horse to water but you can't make it drink." My usual reply was, "No, but you can give it a good hiding in the process."

The face developed at a gradient of one in one which meant it was at forty-five degrees, the steepness of a ladder set up to the roof of a two-storey house. After the chocks were installed the shearer was put on. This shearer differed from the type used in the Rothes as it pulled itself up and down the face on a chain by means of a sprocket wheel with a brake fitted at the rear. The chain had to be extra strong due to the gradient of the face and each chock had five hydraulic legs with steel canopies on top. They were positioned so that four legs formed a square, not unlike a table with the canopies like the flat top. The legs went into a steel box fitted with skids so that they could move into place when required. The fifth leg was situated about three feet in front of this box next to the conveyor. A ram was fitted from the box to the conveyor through the middle of the fifth leg and clamped on to the conveyor. The shearer cut a three foot slice from the face as it travelled up or down and the conveyor was pushed over by these rams. After the conveyor was in position the five legs were lowered and advanced to the conveyor by the pulling action of these rams. The legs were then raised to their new position. This was how the face was stripped, a big difference from using compressed air puggers.

A new loader was put in at the 300 level of the Five Foot to cope with the expected output from the face. All the coal at this time was transported by mine car and taken to the pit bottom by loco. There were large tumblers at the back of the pit, where the coal was emptied into hoppers and then transferred into the skips in the shaft for lifting to the surface. As the Five Foot went into production the stone mines were driving in towards their destination, the Barncraig seam, which was two and a half miles from the pit bottom, out under the River Forth. One day on the backshift while I was in charge of the pit bottom, I had to take a loco jack into the loader to lift a loco on to the rails. I took one of the big Metro Vicks and went in. As I was at the Five Foot the mines phoned out for empties so I took twenty-four empty cars into the mine. The mine loco driver was waiting for me and, taking the race off me, he coupled some full cars on. I asked how many full cars he had and he said twenty-four. With the shunter of the Five Foot loco to assist me, I set off towards the bottom. I moved around the bend before the crossing at the Seven Foot. It went from the left track over to the right and as I was gathering speed, I applied the brakes and then heard the cars bumping together. The loco started skidding and the bumps kept on happening more and more. The alarm bell on the loco started ringing as I was now over the speed limit getting faster and faster. What was I going to do? I was approaching the crossing fast in a wheel locked skid. I released the brakes to allow the wheels to turn then applied the brakes but once more they caused a skid. I did this a couple of times and by now I was on the crossing. I released the brakes, wedged my feet on the front of the loco cabin and held on. The loco went over the crossing and I'm sure it was on two wheels as it sped on to the straight, off towards the Five Foot crossing about two hundred yards away. I tried the brakes once again and they caused a skid once more. I kept trying the brakes on and off, but the loco was skidding towards the Five Foot. This crossing went back over from right to left. I hit it at speed, with alarm bells ringing loud and clear, brakes off, feet wedged, cabin roof scraping the side of the tunnel. I was in a cold sweat but again my guardian angel must have been with me as the loco straightened itself and shot off the crossing on to the straight towards the pit bottom.

It took about three hundred yards to stop. I looked over at the other cabin to see if the shunter was all right, but there was nobody there. I had a sinking feeling in my stomach. I looked up the tunnel to see lights coming towards me, so I started to walk towards them. "You must be mad! Bloody mad!" was all I could hear. It was the shunter along with the other loco driver. "What happened to you?" I asked him.

"I jumped off, that's what happened, you daft bugger." he shouted.

"Wait a minute," I said, "the blasted train was a runaway."

We went and counted the number of cars on the race and found there were fifty and not twenty-four as there was supposed to be - no wonder it ran away!

Between the pit bottom and the Seven Foot in the companion mine, the Cementation Company created a junction and started to drive a heading towards the Seven Foot. I was given this as my area to supervise and carry out the blasting. The drivage was up about sixty yards and one day when I got down to the firing station after charging the face, who should be standing there but Mr Barrie and Bill Kennedy. I coupled up to the exploder and turned the key, but all we heard was a solitary shot going off and not the whole face. "What are you going to do now?" asked Mr Barrie. I replied that I would wait the regulatory fifteen minutes before examining the face and so we waited and then they came up to the face with me. On reaching it all I could see was one little hole away over on the right. "What are you going to do now?" I was asked and it felt like I was back at the mining school. I started to explain what I was going to do when Mr Barrie said, "Don't talk about it, do it." So I split the face and tested both sides - one read high, the other normal. Mr Barrie then started to couple the bad side on to the normal side one at a time, telling me to keep testing until I found the bad one. We eventually isolated one hole which contained the faulty detonator. I managed to get the stemming out of the hole and put in a new detonator. We finished off the wiring up and set off the charges. "There that wasn't too bad, was it Ian?" Mr Barrie said to me before he went away into the sections.

The main mines being developed by the Cementation Company were past the Lower Dysart and Dysart Main seams, passing the Chemiss, Braxton, and the Coxtool seams before reaching the Barncraig. I was employed in the 300 pit bottom area as the Seven Foot had been abandoned, although I could be sent to any area where a deputy was off. In the mine developments the Cementation Company workers were on a four shift system. One of the 170 deputies went off and I was put in until he returned. The shifts were 6 a.m. to 12 noon, 12 noon to 6 p.m., 6 p.m. to 12 a.m., and 12 a.m. to 6 a.m. The changeover was at the face and this meant that, for example, the 6 p.m. to 12 a.m. workers returned to the surface at 1.30 a.m. On a Friday it also meant that you had to return to the pit at 1 p.m. to get your pay. The supervisor of that shift would go up at 9.30 a.m. on the Thursday for materials and would collect everybody's pay, including the deputies'. While I was on the backshift in the pit bottom, I would go up to the surface on the last tow along with the supervisor.

When I went to the 170 drivage I assumed that the system was the same there, but apparently it was not. It seemed that one of the supervisors would not go to the surface for the wages so the drifters went to see their agent. The agent told them that if the Coal Board paid for the time a drifter would spend going to the surface to collect the wages, then he had no objections if he did so. However, the coal board manager said no to this and therefore they were not allowed up. When I arrived at the 170, I didn't know anything about this little dispute. On the Thursday night the supervisor on my shift was a stranger to me, he had been transferred from a pit in Africa back to a position at home. He asked if one of the drifters could take his place to go up for the materials and the wages and, not knowing about the situation, I saw no reason not to let him. The onsetter phoned in asking if I was giving a drifter permission to go to the surface and I said I was. On the Monday morning the usual deputy returned to work so I went back to the 300 level. The undermanager, Jim Glancy, told me that Mr Barrie wanted to see me at the end of the shift and in the meantime I was suspended from deputies' duties. I was speechless. "What for?" I asked.

"For letting the drifter up on Thursday night. So you have to go and clean up the main belt for this shift and for many more I should think."

"No way," I told him, "I am still an official of this mine and as such I'm not going to do any other type of work except that which falls into that category."

He backed down at this and told me to go into the Dysart Main and supervise the shifting of a conveyor, which I duly did. Later that shift, Mr Barrie, along with Glancy, Bill Kennedy, and my favourite overman, who had been transferred from the Rothes, came into the section that I was working in. The only one who spoke to me was Bill and he told me to report to Mr Barrie at the end of my shift.

Mr Barrie was with Glancy in the undermanager's office when I went in. I was told I was off the job and would be demoted to oncost. I asked why and was told, "You let a man out of your section and up the pit to draw wages, including your own. He then came back down and returned to your section."

I said, "That is correct. This is done on these particular shifts every week."

"No it's not - you have just created this precedent against Mr Ludkin's orders."

I argued with them for a considerable time, pointing out what took place in the 300 when I was pit bottom deputy on the backshift, but they wouldn't listen. A while later Mr Ludkin came in and asked why I had started this system. I explained about the backshift in the 300 and what went on with the Cementation Company supervisors. He looked at Mr Glancy and said, "Is this stopped now?" and Glancy said, "I'll see to it after I've dealt with Ian here." Mr Ludkin looked at him, "So! It has been going on during the other shifts and the Cementation agent didn't know anything about it." Whereupon a very humiliated Glancy admitted this was the case.

"Right Mr Barrie you deal with Ian but withdraw the action I demanded happen to him." Then off he went.

"Well Ian," said Mr Barrie after Ludkin had left, "You're cleared, but remember next time you might not be so lucky. Off you go."

I was off the hook, but I would have liked to have been a fly on the wall when the wee man let go at Glancy.

One day as I was in the pit bottom area, Glancy came off the cage along with the chief engineer and asked me to get them a loco with a man riding car as they were going into the Five Foot. When I returned with the car they asked me to come into the Five Foot with them. The chief engineer seemed to be smelling my breath and I wondered what was going on, but they left me and I went on with my inspections.

When I got to the surface that day, Glancy called me into his room. "Ian I believe you have been smoking underground. The chief engineer thinks the same, he could smell it on your breath."

For a moment I was speechless, but then replied, "Wait a minute, Mr Glancy, I do not smoke, I never have done. So how do you explain smelling smoke from me?" I was really mad. "As for your so-called witness, he's only agreeing with you because of who you are. I'll tell you something, I would never report anyone for smoking, I would just flatten them with a mash and then send them up the pit on a stretcher." And with that I walked out. Apparently some engineers had been in the pit bottom with me and they thought the smell was coming from me. What is more likely is that someone had been smoking on the pithead and probably the smell had come down in the air and had attached to my clothes. This was Glancy's way of trying to get me for the last episode regarding the wages.

Thirteen
Seafield, 1966

The developments at the 170 were being driven down towards the 300 level at the grade of the seams, which was one in one, blasting through the solid coal in the Dysart Main and setting in straight cross piece girders fourteen feet long, supported by six feet high legs with clamps holding them together just like goal posts. Only the coal was extracted in the Dysart Main so that the link could be made from the 170 to the 300 more quickly. There was a team of developers coming up from the 300 towards us in the seam and the distance between us was about six hundred yards. The Lower Dysart was also being driven, using ten feet by eight arch girders in the solid coal and rock. I enjoyed blasting this face, putting the last delayed action detonator in each corner with the maximum amount of explosive. When the face went off, the conveyor was left running and the shots blew the material out on to it. When we went back after the shots, the side nearest to the conveyor had only a couple of shovels full to clean out, then it was ready for the girder.

As the dipping tunnels advanced we had a problem with water. A blast pump was installed to clear the face of water before the face could be drilled, but the explosives would get damp and only the part that the detonators were in would go off. ICI who made the explosives sent us a water repellent type to try out. It was slightly larger in diameter than the other type so the drilling pattern had to be changed as well as the amount required to blast the face. One day the undermanager sent for me and introduced me to an explosives expert from ICI, a 'wet behind the ears' graduate. "Take this chap with you," I was told, 'He'll show you how to drill the face and how much explosive to use." I had been using this explosive for more than a week already and knew exactly what was needed. I started to say so but the undermanager told me, in no uncertain manner, that I was to do whatever the ICI chap wanted with no arguments.

I went underground, along with the expert, into the section. On reaching the face he brought out a drilling pattern and instructed the developers to drill the face according to it. He then told me the number of detonators that he wanted and the amount of explosives to put in. He had every hole charged to the maximum. I told him they were too heavy but he said, "I know what I'm doing, so just stem up the holes." After charging the face and coupling it up I retired to the firing station. We started up the conveyor, then I fired the shots. All hell broke loose. The conveyor was almost ripped away from its anchors and was bouncing up and down; there was debris flying all over the place. It was as if a large bomb had gone off, not a developing face. While dodging flying coal, I managed to stop the conveyor and after a while we went towards the face. We got to about forty yards. There we met our first obstacle - girders, which had been blown out from the face, lying on their backs. There were at least fourteen sets of them lying there. The conveyor pans were stacked on top of one another, right up to the roof. "Oh! I think there must have been a fault in the seam to cause this to happen," the so-called expert said, disappearing away up the tunnel and off to the surface, leaving yours truly and the men to salvage the mess. But I got stuck in, along with the developers, and our first job was to get the conveyor working so that the debris could be shifted to allow us to reset the girders.

I eventually got back to the surface to be greeted by the under-manager asking me what I had been thinking of to allow this to happen.

"You told me to do as I was told with no arguments!"

"Within reason," was his reply.

"I'll tell you what", I said, "keep him away from my shift or I won't be responsible for my actions."

"Well, he'll be with you when the face has been cleaned up and secured".

A couple days passed and the developing started once more. As I was talking to my nightshift mate, who should appear but the expert. "Come on then," I told him, getting a warning look from the undermanager. Off we went down the pit and into the section.

Going down to the face I told him to sit, watch, listen and learn. I gave him a drawing of our drilling pattern, with the detonator numbers and the amount of explosives required. After coupling up we retired to the firing station, started up the conveyor, then set off the charges. The noise of the charges going off was a fine healthy sound, music to my ears, then the coal started coming up the conveyor. "That's how it should be done," I told my explosives expert, "Next time listen to the chap with experience of the job." The expert went away to the surface and when I got up that day, the undermanager wanted to know what I had said to him as he had left to return to the ICI works with hardly a word. "That's my secret," was all I said.

I worked there until the link was completed and then I returned once more to the pit bottom area. I worked there for a little while, until a deputy, who had been sent in to the Dysart Main to be in charge of a new compressed air driven machine used for driving up the steep gradients, found the dust and the steepness of the seam too much so we were changed over.

This machine, the Demag, was made by a German company and could develop a face line or a heading at one in one. It consisted of a cutting boom attached to a centre box shape with four hydraulic legs and a canopy on top. Attached to each side were skids containing two hydraulic legs with canopies above them. The centre section also had an apron at the front with a chain conveyor leaning down on to the floor of the seam. The boom was about nine feet long with a drum containing cutting picks on the front. When the centre section was lowered, rams attached to the side skids would push the centre forward. With the drum turning, the picks would enter the coal as the centre advanced. The centre would advance two feet then the legs were pressurised to the roof. When this movement was completed the side legs were lowered. The same rams that pushed the centre up would close, pulling the skids up, alongside the centre section, then they too were pressurised. When all the legs were pressurised the boom started to cut away at the coal face. It cut a swathe fourteen feet wide by two feet deep and six feet high. The coal was taken to a side conveyor by the front chain conveyor, then deposited at the rear where it was transported down the heading by a steel sledge, like a bucket, called a slusher bucket or scraper.

The slusher system was operated by a double drum winch with two steel ropes. The tail ropes passed around a pulley or tail sheave at one end of the face or road and was brought back and attached to the scraper bucket. The pull rope was coupled directly to the front end of the bucket, which was hauled forward and dug into loose coal or stone. When it was full it rode to the discharge point, and when emptied it was drawn back by the tail rope. It was used for loading and transporting coal, or removing and loading stone which would be used to pack a part of the face which had had its coal extracted. The means of ventilating this heading was by an auxiliary fan drawing away from the face. This fan had two purposes, one for ventilation and the other to remove dust from the cutting head. At the rear of the Demag was the power pack, where the compressed air line came in, operating a power pump to work the hydraulics. It also contained the hydraulic oil reservoir. As the machine advanced, straight steel girders set on legs, with clamps, were positioned every four feet.

This heading was called No.1 North Face Line and went up for two hundred yards. At the end of the companion mine which was driven parallel to the main mine and which would eventually have a belt conveyor installed in it, the Cementation Company had driven a rising mine up to the 256 level above the 300 level, which split the seams and allowed access to them. The top road of No.1 North face line was driven out to this heading. Further out they also drove a mine to the 213 level which also split the seams. So there we had the 170 level, then the 213 level, then the 256 level, finishing off at the 300 level. Each coal seam was able to support three coal faces on each side of the main mine and each coal face was two hundred yards long with Shearer coal cutters and Gullick chocks all positioned at one in one gradients.

After the Demag had developed the heading it was dismantled and sent to the surface for overhaul. I was sent into the south side of the Dysart Main to develop the main gate for the face line. On one shift when I went in, the developers were waiting at the explosives bogie, a special bogie that carried two hundred pounds of explosives in four separate cardboard boxes containing fifty pounds each. I usually transferred the explosives from the bogie into steel boxes for the men to carry into the face but on this particular day there were no steel boxes at the bogie. As the face was ready to fire, I let them take in a fifty pound cardboard box, the amount I used to fire the face.

I had just started to charge up the face, when who should walk in but Mr Barrie, along with a government inspector. I quickly put another cardboard box containing the bags of sand for stemming on top of the explosives. The inspector called me over. "Here we go," I thought, "caught red-handed with explosives not in their proper containers." But instead he asked if I could charge up and fire this face with delays of up to No.5 delay, instead of up to No.7 delay as I was currently using. I told him I could do so and he brought out a sheet of paper and a pencil. "Show me," he said, so I sat down and drew a drilling pattern, illustrating the number of delayed action detonators required up to No.5's in the bottom corners. I was then told to write in the amount of charge each hole required, which I did. The inspector studied my drawing and then, turning to the cardboard boxes, he put his hand into the bottom one and drew out a stick of explosive. "Is this the type you are using?" and I nodded because I was speechless. He examined the writing on the side and merely said, "No more than forty-eight ounces in any one hole. Well, thanks: we've got to cut down on the overall time for firing out of solid coal, so your plan is a good one."

With that he walked away, but Mr Barrie said, "Well done, but come and see me when you get to the surface." It looked like I was in trouble again and all the other deputies were betting on what would happen to me. "You'll be cleaning gautons for years to come," seemed to be the favourite prediction.

I arrived on the surface and after giving my report to the oncoming deputy, I went to see Mr Barrie. In his office I found the inspector sitting with him. He spoke first. "Ian, I have looked very closely at your pattern and can see it will work, so once again thank you. I will introduce it to other pits." He then got up and left.

"Now Ian!" Mr Barrie started, "What am I going to do about the cardboard box of explosives?"

"Well sir, there were no steel boxes but the face was ready to fire and I didn't think."

"That's your problem - you don't think and you're too impetuous." I tried to say something more but he held up his hand. "The inspector commented on this, but as you were able to solve his problem satisfactorily, he told me to let you off with a warning. So off you go and count yourself lucky."

I spent a couple of weeks in the south side developing, when once more I was summoned to Mr Barrie's office. What had I done this time, I wondered. When I entered his office he was smiling. "I've a wee job for you at the Randolph Colliery. The Randolph has to drive a surface mine from the Red House power station area down into the Lethamwell seam. Davy Reid is there at the moment, but I want him back here so you go there and take over from him." Sighing with relief, I accepted right away.

This mine, in a field opposite the big electric sub-stations, was going down at a dipping of one in five. The debris from the mine was brought to the surface by means of a steel scraper conveyor, known as a panzer pan, and was stockpiled on a concrete plinth from where it was uplifted once a week by a loader from the Frances along with a couple of lorries. After I fired the face on my first shift there, I got a visit from a very irate operator from the sub-station. Apparently the firing caused all their instruments to go crazy. "Next time you fire, let us know," he said and I agreed to do so.

I spent four weeks at this development until we reached the Lethamwell seam. The manager could not believe it as we were only down about a hundred yards, but looking at the structure of the seam from a drawing it was definitely the Lethamwell. The Randolph men then took over the rest of the link up coming from their side, so it was back to Seafield for me.

Back at Seafield I was sent into the Barncraig section to develop the south side face line. This was being developed by hand: boring and firing the coal, removing it by slusher bucket, and erecting steel square sets as was done at the Dysart. The roof in this section had a band of fossilised mussels about twelve inches thick. These mussels were just like the type found on the other side of the River

Forth at Musselburgh. While doing this we installed the Gullick chocks as we went, removing the square sets and re-using them.

One day, a mate of mine on the shift before me was walking up to the face when he lost his footing and put out his hand to get support. But instead of finding the wall it went into the slusher wheel and three of his fingers were sliced off. He rushed off the face to another deputy, holding out his hand to get it bandaged. But the next thing he knew the deputy was lying at his feet, having fainted at the sight of blood. So there was my mate with three fingers off, trying to revive the deputy. Luckily, some of the developers came off the face and seeing what had happened, they attended to the man's hand. Fortunately, the wheel had only taken off the tip of the pinky and the top joint of the other two, so despite all the blood it was not as bad as it seemed and after a short spell off he was soon back into the fray.

Once the face had been developed we installed the face conveyor, and when that was done we then opened up the end stables to allow the installation of the shearer. I had fired some shots in the bottom stable and went in to examine it when, without any warning, the roof fell in on top of me. It crashed down on to my head, pushing it down between my knees and bending me in two. Next thing I knew I was pushed out away from the face. Had I gone inwards, I would have most likely received a broken neck if not body. So it seems my guardian angel was about once more. I had to go to the hospital where, after X-ray, they fitted me with a neck collar and sent me home. I was to wear the collar for a week or so, but if there were any problems I was advised to come back. A few days later I had to go back as the pain was murder. I saw a consultant who studied the X-ray and told me that some time earlier in my mining career I had chipped the sixth cervical vertebrae and this new wound had opened up the scarred tissue. "Only time will heal it so just wear the collar," he told me and signed me off for a couple of weeks.

When I returned to work the Demag had been overhauled and sent down to drive a heading from the 300 to the 170 in the Chemiss seam. This heading was again steep and the presence of water was an added problem. But we encountered another problem when advancing the machine as it had a tendency to go over to the left for no reason at all. One day as I was guiding the machine into the cutting position, I was sitting below the centre canopy watching the rams to ensure they were moving in together. The operator was kneeling at the controls with the outside legs fully pressurised. Suddenly the whole machine shot backwards, knocking out steel sets as it went. The operator was pushing all the levers up to get the legs to pressurise on to the roof and when they abruptly took hold, the machine stopped dead but I didn't. I flew off the centre section over the power pack and down the heading, landing at the side of the coal. My head was spinning, I was seeing stars, and the breath was knocked out of me. "Take his dust mask off and check his breathing," was the first thing I heard. Then off came my rubber face mask and an anxious face was peering at me in the light of a lamp. I managed to mutter I was all right, but on checking myself I found I had a nice gash down my shin.

I reported the incident to the undermanager who notified the manufacturer. They sent a representative out to find the cause of this problem as there had never been any reports of the machines running away like that. His report said that on studying the area, he felt that the slusher bucket pulling on the return wheel (situated at the rear of the Demag and attached to the side conveyor) as the machine advanced was responsible. Our theory was that the steepness of the heading, along with the wet conditions, caused the rock on the floor to separate, making it unstable and causing the machine to run away. But the rep didn't agree so we got instructions that the slusher must be stopped and the ropes slackened off before the machine was advanced.

The heading started advancing once more and everything went well for a while until one day it ran away again. This time it trapped a deputy's head against the coal, damaging a nerve in his neck. The operator was also trapped and got two broken ribs. The firm still insisted that there was some other factor causing their machine to run away, so we proceeded up the heading slowly as we had to support the back of the machine with anchor props as we were moving up. Once we got up to the 170 level the machine was dismantled and sent away. I heard later that it had been introduced into another pit that had level workings (possibly Kinniel Colliery).

When the machine was sent away, link roads were driven out to the 256 and the 213 levels. One day I went down to the 300 level just before finishing time and I ran into one of my mates. Because the Demag had been dismantled he had been sent to organise the transport and supplies in at the Dysart. He was as white as a ghost and I asked him what was wrong. "There is a man underneath the carriages of the man riding train and I think he's dead." I went along the train and at the fifth carriage I went under to look. The man was on his back and his eyes were open and staring upwards; when I couldn't find a pulse, I realised he was dead. I told my mate to go in to the Dysart Main and send the miners out of the companion mine to the pit bottom. I then went and measured up the locus of the accident for the management and the union investigator and after a short while the ambulance crew arrived along with volunteers to lift the cars off the man and get him out. Once he was released they wrapped his body in canvas and took him out to the pit bottom in a mine car. It was quite a journey. It was likely that the man had tried to board the train as it was being shunted back into the man riding station and had fallen to his death, but nobody was really sure how this random and tragic accident actually happened.

Fourteen
Seafield, 1967 - 1968

The Wellesley Colliery at Denbeath near Methil closed in 1967 and some of its miners were transferred to Seafield. I was still developing the Chemiss heading, and a team of these miners was sent in to back brush the lower section from the six feet high Demag cut and to position twelve feet by eight arch girders. This roadway went from the 256 down towards the 300 level. It was very wet and the roof was faulted. The men had not seen such steep workings. They were a good bunch of lads: Jim Comrie, David Black and George Hunter.

We had a few hairy moments while blasting this road. It would not break off at the supported line but would travel on, leaving large stones hanging dangerously. We had to close off the road at the 300 level so no-one would get hurt. Once the Demag was finished in the Chemiss it was sent to the surface and I was sent to other developments. On the odd occasion when I met Jim Comrie he would always greet me with "Well, Mr Terris" and I would reply, "Well, Mr Comrie." We had a good rapport with one another. He went on to work in power loading after the Chemiss.

On the 9th of September the Michael Colliery went on fire with the loss of nine miners' lives. Apparently a fire started in a section off one of the main roads, setting the conveyor alight which allowed the fire to spread. This section was manned mainly by men transferred from the Wellesley who were not familiar with the escape routes. The fire raged through the workings and could not be put out. Mine Rescue teams went in and brought out the survivors, but they tried in vain to rescue the missing miners and tragically some bodies were never recovered.

After this disaster the Michael Colliery was abandoned. There was still a set of winding wheels and gear at the pithead and pumps still working there until recently as the pumps prevented water flooding the Frances pit which had been on a care and maintenance basis since the strike of 1984 (it is now closed).

After the Michael was abandoned, the men and officials were transferred to other pits and a couple of undermanagers and some overmen and deputies were sent to Seafield. They had a bad habit of saying, "We did this or we did that this way in the Michael" to nearly everything that they were told to do. One day Mr Barrie was going round a section when an overman told him that he did a particular task this way in the Michael. Mr Barrie's comment was, "I thought we were nationalised, but now we are Michaelised" and this phrase was used around the pit for a while wherever a Michael official was.

I was put in charge of a different type of machine, a Dosco Miner. It was a tunnelling machine on level workings which cut through coal and stone. The machine had a cutting boom sitting on a platform and this platform sat on a base which was propelled by crawler chains, like a caterpillar tractor. The boom was about nine feet long with a two feet cutting drum at the front. On the apron of the platform there was a chain conveyor not unlike the Demag's which loaded on to a belt conveyor at the rear which discharged on to the main belt. The size of the drivage was twelve feet by eight and used a special girder. The cutting head would remove two feet on each advance and when four feet had been excavated the cutting head was advanced in four feet to clean up the coal still lying at the face. The whole machine would then be brought back until it was under the last supporting girder. A special arm was then moved from the rear of the boom on to the cutting head. The girder was assembled on this arm and the machine was advanced. As the machine advanced the boom was raised lifting the girder up to the roof and this way no miner had to go under the newly exposed roof. The girder was then set to a centre mark which was put on using a set of three string plumb lines hanging down from the roof and out of the tunnel a bit. I would look through these strings towards the face where the operator would hang my flame lamp on the girder. When I got my lamp sighted through all the strings the girder was at the centre of the road and then it was set in with timber.

These strings were put up by the mine surveyors using their special equipment and were checked once a week and advanced as required. This was the method used to ensure your tunnel was going in the right direction. Some years earlier a mine had been driven under the Forth from Kinneil Colliery at Bo'ness to Valleyfield Colliery in Fife. This mine was a couple of miles long and was driven from both pits towards each other. They used this method to keep their drivages in the right direction and when they broke through, the tunnels were only a couple of inches out.

I then went to the Bowhouse section on the 170 level. A face had been developed in the north side and I was part of the installation squad. I was responsible for the transportation of the chocks into the face from the main mine. We had developed a new type of bogie which was a low loader. The chock sat in between the wheels on this frame close to the rails, so did not get caught in any roof obstruction as it went in. At the face we had built a roller bed consisting of a series of rollers set on metal angle irons. When the chock arrived at the roller bed it was off-loaded using a powered lifting tackle. The fifth leg and canopy were then assembled on to the chock body and it was now ready to be transported down the face and placed in position. A large twin drum haulage had been installed in a recess at the top of the face. The main rope went down the face around a pulley and back up to the top. This rope was attached to the front of the chock while a second rope was attached to the chock's rear and in this way it was transported down the face. A team of developers then put it in position. This seam was also at a one in one gradient.

After the face was installed I stayed as the roads deputy for the area, but if any of the face deputies were off I would take their place. I was the face deputy for a good spell at one time, replacing the usual deputy who was ill, while my pal was acting face overman. The colliery overman, who was superior to both of us, was a Michael man and a bit of a mouth. I was at the bottom stable as the shearer was on the road down. Great care had to be taken in this stable when the shearer was coming in and because of the gradient everybody had to get out in case it ran away or the chain broke. I had witnessed a chain breaking when I was in the Dysart Main and knew the danger. The colliery overman was in the stable shouting at the men to get some of the supports moved so that the shearer would have a quick turn round. The shearer was only a few feet away and he was still getting the men to move the supports. I stopped the conveyor, thus stopping the shearer. "What's wrong?" he roared.

"Out of the stable please," I replied. He shouted to get the conveyor going but I refused. "I'm asking you to get out of the stable."

He started shouting and swearing at me. I then told him to get out or I would send him up the pit. I told him straight. "According to the Coal Mines Act, I am responsible for all persons in my district and that includes you - so move!" He then came over the pans ranting and raving and once he was out of the way I started up the pans and the shearer starting cutting into the stable. It cleared the last bit of coal, but then it shot down at least six feet, knocking out a couple of supports. If he or any of the men had been in the stable they would have been badly hurt, if not killed, and I would have had to answer for this from a witness box in the High Court. The overman's face turned from white to red and he stormed away up the face without a word. I didn't get on with him much after that, but after a while another overman came to the face and I went back to being the roads deputy once more.

This face had a tendency to force the shearer to rise up into the roof as it was difficult to cut the coal on the floor and the shearer would rise up on it. Once this happened it was very difficult to rectify as it usually resulted in the roof caving in. Attempts were made to try and alleviate the problem, but to no avail. Once it got so bad that the manager decided to salvage the chocks off this face and re-develop it by putting a smaller type of chock on a new face fifty yards in from the original one.

I was on the night shift salvaging the face on the last night before the men knocked off for their summer holidays. It was 12.50 a.m. when the colliery overman came to tell me I was needed on the face as there had been an accident. Although it was very wet and water was running down the floor, I got there as soon as I could and found my mate attending to Jim Ednie by bandaging his head. Jim was lying on the face track and had been struck across the legs with the haulage rope. They had been withdrawing a chock when it had jammed and the steel bolt they were using to hold the rope on to the chock had broken. The tension on the rope made it whiplash, striking Jim on the legs and lifting him up in the air. As a result he struck his head on the skids of the chock, splitting it wide open.

When I approached him he was in terrible pain from his legs. I spoke to him but every time anyone came near him he yelled with pain. I have never felt so helpless in my life - here was a man wearing oilskins lying on a wet face at a gradient of one in one. I gently cut off his oilskin trousers to try to ascertain the seriousness of his injuries and I suspected that both his legs were broken below the knee. Every time I tried to remove his wellingtons he screamed with pain. The men came with a stretcher, but how was I to get him on to this? By this time I was soaking as I hadn't had time to put on my oilskins, but I sat down beside him and while talking to him I got the men to place the stretcher above him. Slowly I got him to raise himself up on to the stretcher. He was in agony but we couldn't pull him or try and lift him. I spoke softly to Jim and with my arm round his shoulder he slowly edged up and up until he was completely on the stretcher. The men then carried him down the face, a very hazardous task as there was nowhere to get a good grip on the slippery floor. Eventually we got him to the level of the main gate and I tried once more to remove his wellingtons, but again he was in too much pain. The colliery overman came in with a ampoule of morphine to give Jim a jag to ease the pain, but to our surprise Jim refused it. "When I get to the hospital," he said, "I will have to lie until the jag wears off before they will attend to me. But if I don't take the jag they will treat me right away, so I don't want it."

I made Jim as comfortable as I could, tying his legs together with triangular bandages, supporting them on blankets and covering him as well. We transported him out on a bogie to the material heading. This was where I encountered my next problem - how to get him up two hundred yards at a one in one gradient to the 170 level. We managed to place the stretcher from the first material bogie across on to the second bogie setting it as level as we could. The haulage then pulled us up. I was positioned between the two bogies and cradled Jim's head in the crook of my arm, while holding him on the stretcher to stop him from slipping down. All the way up he was saying "My legs are broken, my legs are broken," and I kept saying "You'll soon be kicking a ball about with your son, you wait and see."

"You're a liar Terris," he said, but he still managed to give a bit of a laugh.

When we got him to the top of the material heading we took him out to the ambulance car. The colliery overman then said he would escort him out to the bottom and up the pit. All the men went away with the stretcher and I was left on my own. I went back into the face, not feeling very happy I can tell you. The union man came in after me so I drew him a plan of the accident with all the measurements. What a way to spend a Friday night, especially Fair Friday.

Jim's legs were indeed broken and he was off for a long time. I was interviewed by a government inspector about the incident.

"Where were you when the accident happened?"

I explained where and what I had been doing before I was told of the accident.

"What time did you pass your men in to your section?"

I told him about 10 p.m.

"You mean to say that you did not see them until the accident?"

I replied that I was on my mid-shift inspection and was in the development before climbing up the face. As I had until 1.30 a.m. to complete my inspection, I was within the time. I had gone down the material heading to check up on supplies for the development, then started my inspection from there. When I left the top, the colliery overman along with the face overman were on their way down the face and they had just crossed over the rope before it whiplashed up the face, striking Jim. The colliery overman said he was away down the face and the face overman was just below the scene of the accident. The funny thing was the colliery overman had immediately gone to get morphine, a strange thing to do if he hadn't seen the incident.

The government inspector said, "As you are the deputy it was your responsibility to see the men as soon as possible. I think you were cutting it a bit fine." He then went on to ask why I had not administered the morphine. I told him I had three reasons: firstly, Jim refused to have any; secondly, he had in my opinion a serious head injury; and last, but not least, I was not certified to administer morphine. The inspector asked why I had not been given this training and I told him it was up to the individual whether they took the training or not, and I chose not to.

The face was redeveloped with smaller chocks. An electronic device was implemented to stop the machine from rising up and cutting into the roof. Sensors would send out a signal between the floor and the roof and the machine was supposed to react to these signals and adjust itself accordingly. It was a partial success, although the wet conditions did affect it from time to time.

Fifteen

Seafield, 1969 - 1975

I spent some time in the Bowhouse section on various deputy duties and then was sent into the 256 level to drive the main gate for the next section. It was going to come out in the retreat system after the No.1 section was worked out (the retreat system was a way of mining whereby roads were driven into the coal seam to pre-determined boundaries and the coal is then extracted in the opposite direction, allowing the roads to collapse). Again I was in charge of a Dosco Miner and again the development was a single road with no escape route so we were only allowed to have ten men inside at the workings.

At the entrance to the roadway at the belt loader there was a board with checks and hooks. When you entered this road you took a check and hung it on a hook. This enabled anyone who came along to know how many men were inside. It would also help, in the event of an accident, to let the rescuers know how many might be trapped or injured.

One day my Dosco operator broke his fingers and went off work. Another man had to take over the controls, but he wasn't happy to do this so I ended up being the operator as well as the deputy. However, it was a task I thoroughly enjoyed doing. When the roadway was driven in its distance we then developed the face. This was done by the conventional way of boring the face and firing it with explosives.

In October 1971, I had to go to the hospital for an operation and was off for about ten weeks. In March or April the following year I took my daughter Janice, now twelve years old, down the pit as a special treat. It was about seven o'clock in the evening when we arrived at the pithead. In the cage her eyes went wide as we hurtled down and, stepping off at the pit bottom, she couldn't believe the height of the roof or how brightly lit it was. We then went around to the man riding station where a locomotive with a car was waiting for us. She felt like royalty, sitting in the train with her dad beside her. We trundled in towards the Dysart Main two and a half miles out under the River Forth. We got in as far as the 213 crossing to find that a material train had come off the rails. The loco drivers and shunters were moving the cars backwards and forwards, putting wooden straps under the wheels to try to get them back on to the track. I told our driver that we would walk the rest. As we approached the crossing and the derailed material cars, Janice spotted a red bogie being pushed up by the loco on to the rails, but it missed and bumped down again. They drew it back across the crossing to try again. "What's in the red bogie, Dad?" she asked. "That's the explosives for the mine driving," I told her. You should have seen her face, it was a picture.

"Explosives?" she asked.

"Yes, but they're quite safe as there are no detonators in them."

We continued going in the main mine until we reached the foot of the 213. We then went up this heading and she was amazed at the amount of water coming down it. On reaching the top we walked into the Bowhouse main gate and into the face where we met Jim McIvor the overman and Bill Reid the deputy. Janice already knew these two men as Uncle Jim and Uncle Bill. As we stood at the foot of the face the conveyors were running and the coal was coming out fast and furious. There was a loud drumming noise coming from up the face.

"What's that?" Janice asked.

"Oh that's the Hurdie Gurdie," Bill replied.

"The what?"

"The Hurdie Gurdie," Bill said once more. Janice looked at me and her Uncle Jim and we laughed.

"It's the shearer coming cutting down the face," we told her and Bill asked if she wanted to see it. She said she did so they climbed up on to the face while I stayed with Jim at the foot. Bill told Janice to keep her head turned away from the machine's drum and look towards the chocks. He didn't want her to be struck by a piece of coal from the picks. She saw this huge machine coming down the face cutting into the coal. It looked enormous, filling the whole space between the pans and the roof. The noise was terrific as the drum smashed its way through the coal. With the noise of this machine and the rattle of the steel chains carrying the coal on the conveyor she was very excited. There was dust everywhere; it got up her nose and in her mouth, what an experience.

Once the shearer reached the bottom stable Bill brought her back off the face. It was too dangerous for a little girl to be about when they were moving the chocks. Also they would be advancing the shearer into its next cutting position, with the drum revolving and throwing up pieces of coal. Uncle Jim placed his dirty hands on her cheeks, leaving coal dust on her face. "Now you look like a miner," he told her.

We left Bill and Jim at the face and returned to the locomotive and car. The driver asked if she had enjoyed her visit. "Very much," she told him, but when asked if she wanted to be a miner like her dad, she said "No thank you, I'll stay at school." I took her to see the rest of the pit bottom and then it was up to the surface and home.

Sometime later I was sent to the Six Foot seam where I was put in charge of a Demag which was electrically operated. We were driving a heading from the 300 up to the 256 level to start with. On this heading we set fourteen feet square sets with an additional leg in the middle. This split the heading in two, one side for the slusher bucket and the other for a material track. A special track was introduced with rails made of box section steel. The bogies had special wheels fitted on the side. These ran inside the box section, making it almost impossible for the bogie to come off the track. This system was called the coolie car system.

In the Dysart Main they had started to mine coal from face lines down below the 300 level. This was called the Dysart Dips and the roads went down at the same gradient as the faces for over six hundred yards. To transport miners to the faces, a large coolie car system was introduced. It was quite an experience to travel on it. The bogies sat on the rails at a gradient of one in one and inside the man riding cars the seating was like a hammock in that when you climbed in you were suspended on belting lying on your back. I once saw a similar system in the Llechwedd Slate Caverns in Blaenau Ffestiniog, North Wales.

At the heading we had to attach guide rails to the centre legs of the slusher bucket to keep it in its track. These were ordinary rails drilled and bolted together to prevent the bucket from catching and dislodging them. One night as we were cutting, the bucket caught the end of the last guide rail and bent and buckled it as well as knocking out the square sets. It was a mess but fortunately for us the roof was good and did not come down. We managed to reset the square sets but could do nothing about the guide rails. They had to be left to the dayshift to sort.

The next night I returned to discover that the surface onsetter had been killed. He had gone on to the cage to put some boxes of machine picks on its floor. The winding engine man did not see him and the winder was set on automatic which meant that when the onsetters on both the surface and pit bottom signalled the cage away, it moved off automatically. The onsetter was stepping off the cage when the pit bottom signalled and the cage moved off at a speed of forty feet per second. He was caught between the shaft and the cage and was decapitated. His body fell down the shaft and had to be recovered by the shaftsmen.

Mr Barrie was in the deputies' meeting room. He was in his civilian clothes and wearing a soft hat. He started on at me about the carry-on the night before - why had I not obeyed his instructions regarding the guide rails? Didn't I know they had to be kept up with the drivage? None of this had anything to do with the poor onsetter. He was going on and on but I just stood there, thumbs in my belt, looking down at him and thinking about the dead man. I had known him in the Rothes and spent many a Saturday night piece time in his cabin when we were on the weekend inspections. I never uttered a word and he called over our union man, Jim Hutcheson. "Tell him! Tell him to do as I say!" Mr Barrie was shouting. Jim looked at me and could see that my eyes told a story. "He will Mr Barrie. Won't you, Ian ?" I said nothing and then turned on my heel and went away to the lamp cabin to get my lamps before going down the pit.

The Demag reached the 256 level and was dismantled to be brought down the heading. One of the side skids had been manoeuvred out on to the heading and was secured with a steel girder to prevent it from moving down the heading. The slusher ropes came up bolted together and after separating they were to be attached to the skid. As I was pulling on the rope, I was holding on to the skid with one hand and the rope with the other. I asked for more slack but for some unknown reason the chap at the front pulled away the girder. The skid then started to move and as I was holding on to the rope as well as the skid, I was getting stretched in opposite directions. I let go of the rope, but still held on to the skid. Picture this - a seven feet skid weighing about a ton gathering speed down a one in one heading, with an idiot sliding behind on his bum trying to hold it back. I eventually took a grip of myself and let go and the skid thundered down the heading until it crashed through the belt structure and finished up in the haulage. The operator of the haulage had jumped out when he heard it coming and fortunately no-one was hurt except for my rear end and my pride. Once again, Mr Glancy was not at all pleased with me.

The Six Foot South Face Line was developed and started to produce coal. This face had a more modern ranging drum shearer. It had the normal cutting drum at one end with a ranging drum on an arm at the other. This second drum cut out the top stable thus reducing the need for boring and firing with explosives.

During my time in the Six Foot I had a variety of duties once again, from roads deputy, power loading deputy and sometimes even as acting overman. There was one particular incident which still sticks in my mind. I was on the roads, as well as firing the bottom stable, the advance brushing and the back brushing. I was sitting out at the howf with the colliery overman when a message came over the D.A.K. system. (This was a communication system that connected the face lines with a control centre on the surface, as well as individual parts of the section. Every power loading face had a series of these D.A.K.'s situated every fifty yards up the face line, fixed to the face conveyor.) The message that came over sent a shiver down my spine: "There's a man trapped beneath the shearer."

The shearer was at the top of the face, just below the top stable. We set off up the steep material heading as fast as we could, then we ran along the top road to the face. When we got there, we surveyed the scene. The man was lying underneath the ranging drum. He was not badly hurt although there were cutting picks sticking into both his legs. The small toe on his left foot had been cut off along with his boot's steel toecap. Worst of all there was a pick pressing into his stomach, just at his belly button. Apparently, when the machine had reached the top stable they had cut the stable. Then they moved the machine back down the face to change the cutting picks before going back down. They turned the drum round by switching it on and off and while doing this the man slipped on the steep gradient and went under the drum. Fortunately, the arm had been raised slightly, leaving a gap between the drum and floor or else the accident would have been more serious, perhaps even fatal.

The top stable deputy had administered morphine, but the man was still in pain and shock. The face electrician along with the face engineer opened up the interior of the machine and removed a part called a spider. This part operated the turning mechanism of the drums. The machine could now be switched on and the arm raised. But the man would not let them switch it on and would not accept their assurances that it was totally safe. I didn't blame him, I probably would have done the same. We then had to raise it using chains coupled on to the shearer and on to the fifth leg of the chock and put in wedges of wood underneath to secure it above him. The man was actually telling us when we could get another wedge in place. A rope was placed around his shoulders so that he could be pulled clear whenever the opportunity arose and after what seemed like an eternity we had enough room and the man was dragged out.

After rendering first aid to his wounds we put him on a stretcher and carried him out the tail gate, down the material heading and out to the waiting ambulance car. We were actually on our road out from the face when we met a doctor and nurse sent down the pit from the Victoria Hospital. After checking the man, we continued on out to the car and off to the pit bottom. At the surface there was an ambulance waiting at the shaft and the man was taken off to the hospital. Mr Paterson, our general manager, was also waiting there. He thanked us all for our efforts and told us we could go home and our shift would be paid for. I explained to him that I had left my detonator bag (containing around a hundred detonators) underground and I would have to go back down to get it, but he told me to go and that the overman would bring it up with him at the end of the shift. So I went and got washed and changed, and then stopped in at the Otter's Head for a couple of pints before going home. What a day.

From 1970 I had been attending Cowdenbeath Technical College one day a week to obtain the City & Guilds Coal Mine Technician certificate. I had a friend there who was a deputy in Comrie Colliery, Oakley, called Marvin Jago. We were rivals, always trying to better each other. The first year I came out top of the class and was given a book token. The next year Marvin and I were very close in the marking. The maths teacher read out Marvin's mark. It was ninety-nine percent and he was jumping with joy. "Beat that, Terris," he shouted at me. The teacher then read out my mark - one hundred percent. Marvin went spare but I was top of the class again. The third and final year we had a class test and I came top again.

There was another deputy from Seafield in our class who also worked beside me in the Six Foot section. We were both under the supervision of Jimmy Glancy. One day I met up with Glancy on his rounds. "You're some boy," he said.

"What do you mean?"

"Well, I asked George how he was getting on at college and he told me he's top of the class, which doesn't say much for you as he's not the brightest deputy that I've got."

"That's funny," I said "I've been given the book tokens every year, so for someone who's not top of the class that's a clever thing to do, isn't it."

Glancy was put out. "The lying git," he said, referring to George, "Wait 'till I see him."

On the 11th of May, 1973, I went to Dunfermline to sit my external exams for the certificate. As I was travelling there in the morning, a report came over the radio that there had been a large cave-in at Seafield. I immediately thought of my mate Bill Reid's section as they were going through bad roof conditions at the time, but it turned out to be the Dysart Main D22 face.

The incident had occurred the previous evening at around 6.45. The fall was six and a half feet to eight feet high and extended from power support No.90, which remained upright and pressurised to the roof, to support No.155 which also remained upright and pressurised to the roof. All the supports in between had toppled over with the exception of supports 152, 153 and 154 which remained upright. The length of the fall, which was the full thirty feet width of the excavation, was about 210 feet. A statement made by one of the men who was trapped was as follows: "The whole roof slid down the hill taking the chocks and almost everything with it. The roof in the waste was bursting and I saw the chocks above me starting to topple over. I must have turned to hide myself as that is the last thing I remember. I must have been knocked unconscious or something until I came to myself and found we were completely buried."

Colliery overman A. Bell and the face overman R. Stewart inspected both sides of the fall but the D.A.K. system had been knocked out of action so they could not ascertain the full extent of it. Shortly after 7 p.m. Bell reported to the surface control centre that a heavy fall on D22 extended from power support 90 to about power support 150 and that nine men were trapped. While the undermanager and the deputy manager were travelling in they met a stretcher party carrying miner J. McCartney who miraculously had escaped unaided from the centre of the fall by walking through the waste behind the powered supports to the tail gate roadway. McCartney gave the approximate location of some of the trapped men and confirmed that they were alive. At approximately 10.45 p.m. the first body was found at support 115 and identified as my friend Jimmy Comrie. Nearby, J. Henderson was calling for help and was released from within the structure of a support and placed on a stretcher at around 12.30 a.m. Oxygen was administered from a reviving apparatus but unfortunately he died.

Angus Guthrie, who had been one of my wood laddies on the Demag at the Chemiss, was found dead but his body could not be recovered and brought to the surface until the 17th of May. The body of the leading man, Thomas Kilpatrick, was not recovered until the 6th of June. It was located sixteen feet from the waste side of the conveyor near support 109.

The official inquiry into the incident concluded that the fall started near power support No.90 when the roof beds in the waste broke down heavily and overran several power supports on the face line at a point where there were natural slips in the roof. Bed separation of the immediate roof strata had already taken place at a well defined smooth parting six and a half feet to eight feet above the seam, and the effect of the first fall was to release the detached roof which broke over the coal head and collapsed so that large blocks of roof stone slid down and reeled out the supports, pushing them downhill and backwards into the waste. There followed a progressive collapse of the roof on the rise side. I knew all of the men who were killed and at some time they had all worked with me in the developments.

There are several stories told about that fatal backshift. One was of two miners, one of whom was trapped across his chest while the other lay on top of him with severe facial injuries. When the rescuers reached them, they could find no sign of life in the miner on top so they laid him to the side. They set about lifting debris off the other man and had to cut through some of the hydraulic hoses to free him. Eventually they got him free and on to a stretcher and were about to take him out when the lad lying at the side started to groan. The laying aside of his body must have started him breathing again. Quickly, the rescuers put him on a stretcher and got him off the face.

The other man was then taken out but on the way out he asked them to stop. He thanked them for their efforts and then died. It was very tragic and the men were all really upset. The second man was taken to the hospital with a fractured skull as well as other serious injuries. He never worked underground again.

So, it was with a heavy heart that I sat the exams that day, worrying about my mates at Seafield. I actually passed with credits which surprised me. This qualification allowed me to go to Kirkcaldy Technical College on a sandwich course which would lead towards gaining the Higher National Certificate. I alternated four weeks at the Tech with four weeks at the pit and because I was on this course I was more our less put on special duties.

During the time I had been in various sections of the pit, a stone mine had been driven away from the 300 main mine. This stone mine went in for about a mile before turning and running parallel to the main mine. It cut through the same seams as the 300 main mine, going in as far as the Barncraig. I was sent in to drive a heading with a Demag up the south side of the Barncraig to the 170 level. Another Demag was developing the north face, putting on the chocks as it went. One day as I sat with the other face developing deputy, the undermanager for this area came in for an inspection. After he had completed the inspection he came out to where Pete and I were sitting writing up our reports. He sat on a transport bogie and took off his boot. As he was emptying the dross out he was roaring at Pete about the lack of clevises on the face. These were anchor pieces fitted on to the steel pans to which the centre ram of the Gullick chocks were attached. These clevises had been getting changed in the D22 and they were reported as having a possible connection with the accident in this face line. Pete tried to explain that the reason was due to the lack of delivery of material from the surface. "I don't care," this idiot kept shouting, and then he threw his boot at Pete. He missed and then told Pete to bring it over to him. I told him it was a good job he had not thrown it at me.

"What would you have done?" he shouted at me.

"I would have thrown it back, but only harder and with a better aim," I replied, "You would have been chewing it." He got up and stormed out the section.

It was during 1974 that Joe Gormley, president of the NUM, took on the might of Ted Heath's Tory government by calling a national strike in the coal mines. Everybody came out on strike and the three day week was introduced along with power cuts. Heath then called a general election which he lost to Labour. The miners then returned to work and everything went back to normal. Meanwhile, I sat my first year exam and passed into the next year, but by this time I had decided to leave the mining industry. I applied to go on a training opportunities scheme at Stowe College in Glasgow to study for a certificate to become a work study ('time and motion') engineer. I left Seafield at the end of September 1974 and started at Stowe the following month. I finished the course and began a new job as a work study assistant with Fife County Council in

January, 1975.

I felt sad about leaving the mines, but apart from my short-lived career on the buses, I had never worked in any other industry and I felt I needed a new challenge. I eventually became a management services officer with the council and stayed in this job for twenty-one years.

I never regretted the change, although I still look back on my days in the mines with a great deal of pride. When I left school I had no qualifications. I was told I was only a plodder and would never amount to anything - but I did what I wanted to do and, looking back, I think I proved them wrong.